It's the EconoME, Stupid

The Cause and Solution to Many of Our Difficulties

Gregory A. Gull, has extensive experience working in business and industry, spanning the full spectrum of an enterprise from research and development to advertising. This diverse experience affords him a uniquely integrative perspective and critical insight on business, leadership, quality and organizational design/re-design (see www.forprogressnotgrowth.com). In 2005, he was listed among Executive Excellence's Top 100 Thought Leaders. He holds a Ph.D. in Organizational Studies and an M.A. in Statistics.

It's the EconoME, Stupid

The Cause and Solution to Many of Our Difficulties

Gregory A. Gull

Contents

PROLOGUE

In an effort to explore the thinking and theory behind the essence of capitalistic political economy, we've imagined bringing back Adam Smith to help us better understand his thinking on human nature and also to enable us to go beyond the body of knowledge that was believed to be representative of "the way things are" at the time that he wrote *The Wealth of Nations*. It is hoped that through this discussion we will gain an appreciation of the underlying assumptions on which our current system of economics is based. We also hope to consider how things might be different if what we know today was known then and whether this difference would change our economic system and/or the perception of the role economics plays in our lives and in the management of our organizations.

It is hoped that through the reading of this exchange between Smith and his interlocutor you will begin to understand that it is time to recognize the need to change the why, what, and how of business. That it is time to acknowledge that the assumptions that underlie modern management and organizational theory and practice—that all things are independent, that the whole is equal to the sum of its parts, that all actions/behaviors are externally initiated, that our purpose in life is to amass wealth, and that unlimited growth is not only possible but our guiding principle— no longer serve our best interests. Nothing would be worse than to maintain the status quo, if by "best interest" we mean: best for our personal individual development as human beings and best for those who will live beyond our time. To perpetuate current reality is to cast humankind aside for the allure of transitory material gain—for the sake of a few bucks. To be responsible beings, we must no longer put material worth ahead of human value. Societal wealth is only a small part of our well-being.

The Thinking Behind the System

Questioner: Dr. Smith, I want to thank you for coming forward to enable us to speak with you and to explore your thinking with regard to the nature of humankind in relation to *The Wealth of Nations*.

Dr. Smith: Thank you for conceiving me here. As you may know, my publisher and my friend and colleague the English philosopher David Hume felt *The Wealth of Nations* was an important work, yet we didn't expect it to be so popular. You know, it is a very difficult book to read, for it requires a lot of attention as a result of its analytical style. But I've always wondered what affect the book would have on man and society.

Q: Dr. Smith, if you could, please try to refrain from use of the words "man" or "mankind' when referring to our species. Nowadays, we've become very aware of the discriminatory implications of such terms and so we use the gender-free form, "humankind."

S: OK, I'll try to be more inclusive when choosing words.

Q: Thank you. If you would, Dr. Smith, briefly describe your philosophical orientation.

S: Well, I guess you could say that I tend to be aligned with a group of philosophers that includes Hutcheson, Turnbull, Hume, Ferguson, and Stewart, who advance the belief that man, sorry, I mean people, do not exist as isolated beings but rather in a social context. Further, I suppose you could say that I am an empiricist in the tradition of Sir Francis Bacon and also—following the work of Sir Isaac Newton—believe that there are natural laws that govern all actions or behaviors of people in society. With respect to this, I hold that there is indeed a Divine Plan that is meant to unfold through the propensities and passions endowed to humankind by God. Although I believe the Divine Plan to be rational, it is not always known to the individual as he acts on his passions and propensities. Additionally, the individual is an entity, whereas society is merely the summation of all the individuals and hasn't a character of its own. Therefore, the behavior of the collective is reducible to individual behaviors.

Q: Excuse me, but are you saying that you are an individualist?

S: Yes, in a sense I am an individualist, but I also believe that we are influenced by others in society, or more specifically, by their view of us. I guess that would make me a moderate individualist.

Q: Dr Smith, it seems as though your theory of political economy is grounded in the nature of humankind. Is this true?

S: Very much so. I believe that the science of humankind provides a solid foundation for all other sciences.

Q: And how did you acquire this knowledge of humankind?

S: Through the only way that is valid, by observation and experience, of course. My knowledge of people is empirically derived and therefore scientifically valid.

Q: Briefly then, based on your empirical investigations, how would you describe, characterize, or explain human behavior?

S: People are not motivated by reason, but rather by passions and sentiments.

Q: Could you elaborate a bit more?

S: Human beings experience three types of passions—selfish, social, and unsocial—and all three are driven by the pursuit of pleasure and the avoidance of pain in the moment. The selfish passion addresses the fact that every individual is more interested in what concerns himself than in what concerns others. The social passion has to do with people's propensity for what I've termed "fellow-feeling." By this I mean individuals desire the approval of their fellow human beings. We naturally seek the approval of others and correspondingly desire to be worthy of their approval. And finally, unsocial passions have to do with sentiments that do not engender the approval of others, such as hate and envy.

Q: I read where you said, "every man . . . is much more deeply interested in whatever immediately concerns himself than in what concerns any other." Is this a fair representation of what you believe to be the most important or dominant of the three passions?

S: Yes. I contend selfish passion, the propensity for satisfying one's self-interest, is most significant in influencing an individual's behavior. Even social passion is affected by an individual's self-serving desire to be approved by others; that is, for selfish reasons individuals have a desire to do what ought to be approved of by their fellow human beings. So it isn't that an individual is interested in others, just in others' approval of himself. Again self-interest is the driving force.

Q: Well I suppose, now and then, I've heard "what's in it for me" when people are asked to do this or that. But, are you saying that we are all naturally selfish?

S: Well, when I say selfish, I mean we have concern for personal interests; the propensity for each individual to seek to better his own condition. Human beings are predisposed to use their capacities for reason and imagination to improve themselves materially.

Q: So you are equating self-interest—selfish passion—to the natural desire to better one's own condition—to take care of oneself?

S: Yes, it is aligned with self-preservation, and furthermore, it is part of the Divine Plan. Endowed with selfish passion each individual naturally acts toward bettering his condition and, without actually intending to do so, improves the welfare of society.

Q: How so?

S: Society is nothing but the sum of the actions of each individual—it is nothing apart from what each individual separately contributes to it. So, if each improves materially, then it stands to reason that society will also be better off.

Q: But wouldn't an individual solely concerned for improving his situation be likely to do harm to another? How could society be better off given this negative consequence?

S: This is where the influence of the social passion surfaces. Connected to our selfish desire is our need for the approval of others. People will be restrained because of their concern for realizing the approval of their fellow human beings; and it is this need that controls self-interest in a way that affords harmony and the greater good to society.

Q: So what you are saying is that our self-interest restrains our selfishness.

S: I'm not sure I understand what you've just said.

Q: It is in our self-interest to better our condition and to realize the approval of others; the latter constrains the means by which we seek the former. So our personal (self) interest turns back onto itself to control our selfish behavior.

S: Oh, now I understand. Yes, that's right.

Q: Isn't it then all about pleasure and pain! Satisfying our self-interest provides pleasure. Not receiving the approval of others provides pain—something we avoid. Our desire to maximize our pleasure directs us to better our condition in a way that avoids the pain of disapproval.

S: Moreover, in the Divine Plan, each individual's purpose is to enhance his condition materially—each should seek to maximize his pleasure. Seen in this light, self-interest is the engine of all behavior; that is, it is the cause of the industriousness of humankind, and (in turn) the engine driving the economic growth in society.

Q: It seems that the underlying theme—apart from self-interest—is that people are unknowingly led to improve the welfare of society. Are you intimating determinism as a part of human behavior?

S: Well, yes, determinism is a part of human behavior to the extent that the Divine Plan determines humankind's purpose, along with passions and behavioral tendencies consistent with this purpose.

Q: What you are saying is that an individual is a fixed, constant entity whose reason for being is to maximize personal pleasure by bettering his material condition, which unintentionally also enhances the welfare of society.

S: Now you can understand why in economic exchange our motivation is to advance our position materially.

Q: So, economic exchange would be considered successful if our situation is materially better than it would be if we had not engaged in such activity.

S: Yes, and not only are we better off, we also gain the admiration of others.

Q: That's your fellow-feeling and social-passion concept at work.

S: Yes. We absolutely share a fellow feeling with those of wealth and position. However, we not only admire and revere them, we also—at times—envy them. Further, we also have a tendency for disdain and to detach ourselves from the poor and downtrodden.

Q: Are you saying that we gain and give respect based on what we or others have managed to acquire—not on who we/they are? Are you saying that it is our nature to be externally or materially referenced?

S: Yes.

Q: So, how does this relate to your idea of economics?

S: Well, because every person lives by exchanging one thing for another, economic order emerges when each individual seeks to better his condition in the exchange. Each taking from nature—using what is naturally given—to satisfy his self-serving interests. My economics recognizes that everyone in society sustains himself or herself by exchanging the product of his/her talents with that of another. And remember in so doing, each contributes to the welfare of society.

Q: All part of the Divine Plan?

S: Yes, each is competing, yet guided—as if by invisible hands—to serve the greater good.

Q: Then what is the reason for exchange: subsistence, material gain, or the greater good?

S: Material gain, of course. Might I remind you of what I wrote in *The Wealth of Nations*: "It is not from the benevolence of the butcher, the brewer or the baker that we expect our dinner, but from the regard to their own interest."

Q: I still can't help but think that selfishness can do harm. Wouldn't an economics system in which the intent of the exchange is to be of service to others and society at large be better?

S: Are you suggesting an altruistic exchange?

Q: No, not altruistic in the strictest sense, but an exchange in which all parties are seeking to serve each other in a way that delights. We are not looking to maximize the gain of one but optimize the gain of all. Wouldn't society be better off with such an arrangement?

S: No. What you describe would not be consistent with the Divine Plan. You'd be inhibiting the free expression of self-interest. I am not saying that the butcher, the brewer, and the baker would not provide good products. But rather, it would be in their self-interest to do so, otherwise they would not gain materially.

Q: So, the intent is to satisfy their self-interest, but not to provide good products. The good product happens unintentionally as a result of their self-interest?

S: Yes, that is right.

Q: So benevolence has no place in economic relationships?

S: Benevolence, no: cooperation, yes!

Q: Wait, I thought you said that economic exchange is grounded in competition.

S: Cooperation is naturally required for each to realize the advantage of self-interest. Economic exchange cannot take place in a vacuum of self-interest. That is, our individual interests can only be met in an atmosphere of cooperation.

Q: How can you cooperate if your only interest is your individual self? How can people work together, if each is concerned more for his or her own personal interest?

S: Well, I believe they can. Perhaps we can look at it this way. Consider that in an economic exchange you are playing a game, and for the game to continue each must cooperate with the rules of the game; otherwise the game would lose order and dissolve into chaos. Cooperation among individuals is essential, even if each is seeking to further his own personal interests.

Q: So you aren't cooperating with each other, but rather with the rules of the game! For example, if the rules of the game say that you are to be fair in your efforts to destroy each other—as in the game of war—then you would be cooperating in each others destruction.

S: Let's get back to the butcher, brewer, and baker. What I am saying is that these merchants are dependent on other's approval for their material gain and therefore they must cooperate with them and avoid being greedy.

Q: But cooperation is not dependence, it is interdependence. Being cooperative does not mean that you see the other as instrumental to your own end—that's manipulative.

S: Yes, very much like what the Physiocrats advance: They see that everything is intertwined and interrelated. This is what I am talking about when I say an individual's material gain is dependent on other's approval of the individual's actions. It's all consistent with the Divine Plan, which states that following our endowed propensities of selfish passion and fellow-feeling unknowingly leads us to more wealth in society.

Q: So you aren't advocating helping others through economic exchange.

S: No, not directly. Attend first and foremost to your self-interest and eventually, and unintentionally, everyone will benefit. However, what I do advocate is not doing harm in the transaction. Not being benevolent does not mean that you must necessarily be malevolent.

Q: Cooperation being connected to interdependence implies that each participant in the economic activity must recognize that there is a mutual relationship among individuals.

S: Yes, I agree: Beneficial economic relationships cannot be purely adversarial, because economic exchange necessitates cooperation. In fact, people have a natural propensity for cooperation toward mutual benefit. In this way we each can use our unique skills and contribute to the overall productivity of society–which is the basis for division of labor. Here again selfish and social passions are interconnected.

Q: I would contend that "purely" as a qualifier to "adversarial" is misleading. For long-term sustainability individuals must not be adversarial. Complete collaboration is essential.

S: But, in competing for greater material wealth, individuals must play fair.

Q: Are you saying that competition for material gain must be restrained?

S: Yes.

Q: I thought that self-interest expressed through selfish passion and social passion was self-correcting.

S: Not entirely. Human beings are not capable of self-command or self-control. Individuals require external forces to keep them within the boundaries of fair play.

Q: You are not advocating government control of economic activity, are you?

S: No, not at all. I think any regulation that inhibits an individual—restricting his or her personal liberty—to satisfy the individual's self-interest would be detrimental to the welfare of society.

Q: Then what are you saying?

S: We need not have rules to govern economic activity, but we do need government to enforce rules of morality and fair play. What is required is a system of justice that would ensure fair play but not interfere with or regulate economic exchange. My position on this goes back to my earlier statement that we ought not be benevolent in economic affairs, nor should we be malevolent.

Q: So your economic theory seeks to create a just economy, not a benevolent one.

S: Yes. I oppose benevolence in economic affairs, for it is dishonorable to depend on the good nature of another person. In economic exchange we ought not take an interest in the interests of those with whom we engage in transactions. That is, there must be nontuism in economic transactions.

Q: Nontuism? I am not familiar with this term, what does it mean?

S: It is when we work together yet don't concern ourselves with each other's interests or needs. We should only be interested in others to the extent that our self-interests are served.

Q: So getting back to our discussion of cooperation, your sense of cooperative behavior is an instrumental one, is it not?

S: When I speak of cooperation I am speaking of nontuistic cooperation.

Q: Therefore the rules of justice are the minimum requirements: They are all that is needed for society to materially prosper—do *no harm* but not *do good* is the order of the day.

S: Yes, economic order will be realized when individuals act with restrained self-interest—restrained by the rules of justice. When self-interest is unrestrained, then greed develops and we know that greed is destructive.

Q: Isn't getting it all for yourself the epitome of self-interested behavior?

S: Not in economic affairs, for there would be nothing to exchange. It is only through the exchange of the produce of capital, land, and labor that wealth can be increased. Everything for me and nothing for others is a recipe for destruction and the depletion of wealth, not its growth.

Q: So, in your economics you maintain that all that is required is that the individual's natural propensity to pursue his or her selfish interest be restrained so as not to harm others.

S: Yes, that's right.

Q: But if this economic theory is consistent with the Divine Plan, then why must there be external restraint? Shouldn't the Divine Plan be perfect?

S: Remember, we are endowed with unsocial passions.

Q: So why would the Divine design in imperfection? ... Never mind. Then what you are saying is that people acting on their own interests for material gain has both positive and negative consequences— unintended social outcomes, as you might say.

S: This also relates to a phenomenon we mentioned earlier, the invisible hand. If each is afforded the liberty to pursue his individual self-interest, then the mechanism of competition in the market will impartially regulate economic activity in such a way as to promote lower prices, jobs, and economic growth. These positive, societal-level outcomes are not intended by individual self-interested economic actors; they naturally trickle down or occur as a result of capitalists freely acting on self-interest.

Q: Are you saying that the invisible hand acts as a governor to the engine of self-interest?

S: Yes, precisely that. But the phenomenon of the invisible hand requires fair competition, where no one has an advantage over others and everyone has full knowledge.

Q: But this is never the case! Dr. Smith I would like to ask you one more question before we bring this very informative discussion to a close.

S: By all means please ask.

Q: In *The Wealth of Nations* you state, "labor is irksome." What do you mean by this?

S: I mean that labor is a brutish endeavor and that the only reason to engage in it is for material gain. It is a sacrifice one makes for income.

Q: Dr. Smith, did you sacrifice to write *The Wealth of Nations*? Given your surprise over its popularity; in fact, assuming it wouldn't be widely read, it seems that you didn't write it for income. Do you engage in your intellectual endeavors because of the monetary gain they provide or because you find it interesting?

S: No, not really! I find it interesting and enjoy my work.

Q: Why couldn't–and shouldn't–everyone have the same opportunity as you, to engage in interesting work that brings them joy?

S: Well that's not the way it is! Society naturally has three classes, and one of these is the labor class. It is not likely that each individual will realize his or her betterment, let alone enjoyment in his or her labor. In fact, I would venture to say that it will rarely be the case that individuals will accomplish this.

Q: I thought it was all consistent with the Divine Plan.

S: Actually, there is a little bit of deception involved in the pursuit of self-interest. The better condition we've come to believe we will get is rarely realized. But nevertheless it keeps us forever trying to be materially better off–it causes us to be industrious.

Q: And for whose benefit?

S: Society's.

Q: But recalling what you stated early in our discussion, society is not an entity, only individuals are. So does this mean that societal benefit is but the sum of each individual's benefit? Therefore, if, as you say, it is rare that individuals will realize the wealth and societal rank that they imagine, then how can the sum across all individuals turn out positive?

S: Those who benefit far outweigh those who don't.

Q: So those who don't realize benefit sacrifice for those who do?

S: Well, yes, and in total society is better off.

Q: Well, it might be instructive if we just took a moment to observe some of the effects that the unbridled pursuit of greater and greater wealth has provided.

Dr. Smith, if you were to look back over the last few hundred years and compare then to now, what would impress you about the effects of your system of political economy (i.e., capitalism)?

S: Well, to begin, that my theory of political economy did create wealth. In fact, the application of my theory has created a tremendous amount of wealth—has it not?

Q: It no doubt has, as evidenced by the fact that the United States is one of the most powerful economic nations in the world, with a gross domestic product (GDP) that continues to trend upward. Moreover, other countries that have embraced capitalism have seen wealth accumulate as well. Capitalism is spreading worldwide, like wildfire, with a tremendous amount of wealth created.

S: Unfettered self-interest has done what I knew it would do—create wealth unmatched before in history. How divine!

Q: Also, what you foresaw as remote has in fact been showing signs of developing.

S: What is that?

Q: You had predicted that as a result of the limits of natural resources, capitalism would find that the rate (in growth) of profits would decline. Early in the 21st century many companies are outsourcing labor to foreign lands—lesser developed countries—in an effort to reduce labor costs and increase profits.

S: But I also said that unintentionally the growth in material wealth would permeate throughout society. And with GDP growing unrelentingly, isn't society better off?

Q: Yes and no. According to U.S. census data, the family poverty rate has been hovering at just about 10% since 1980. Since, according to your invisible hand theory, wealth trickles down, wouldn't you have expected that poverty (especially in one of the most industrialized countries in the world) to have nearly disappeared? We have this tremendous material prosperity; it's just that it is not optimally distributed. What John Stuart Mill envisioned, the elimination of classes as a result of each individual pursuing his self-interest, never materialized.

Giving this a bit more thought, we realize that poverty and wealth are the two sides of the same coin—they depend on each other. Accordingly all we have are people striving to acquire and accumulate more. The resultant distribution of wealth is quite uneven with no evidence to suggest a movement toward a fairer balance—trickle down doesn't!

So who is really better off?

S: Society as a whole. As I noted earlier, those who benefit far outweigh those who don't.

Q: What self-interest is doing is widening the gap between the rich and the poor. It seems that those with wealth get wealthier.

The fact of the matter is that success in the competitive game of material self-satisfaction is autocorrelated; winning today increases your chances of winning tomorrow. So, as previously stated, trickle down doesn't!

So, what else impresses you?

S: I see that Frederick Taylor was able to expand the idea of division of labor and apply it for greater productivity in a business enterprise.

Q: Yes, he synthesized your thinking with that of Jeremy Bentham's in developing a scientific method of management. Not only did he apply the concept of division of labor, he also linked material self-interest of the individual worker to the productivity goals of the enterprise—management of and by the numbers.

S: By operationalizing the management of material self-interest in the business enterprise, Taylor seems to have successfully translated the theory of economics into an aligned theory of management of the firm. In so doing, he has contributed to the industriousness of labor.

Q: No doubt, the industriousness of people, as measured by material wealth, improved.

But what if people are more than economically driven? What if the assumption of economic-man is false? How much more industriousness could have been realized?

S: Your questions are pure speculation, for the empirical evidence of history shows that people are indeed, by their nature, economically driven. Look what has been realized by people following their selfish passions. It must be so, for the amount of wealth created is beyond expectation. How can it be otherwise!

Q: What if, by nature, people are adaptable to the conditions within which they exist?

S: I'm sorry, I don't follow you.

Q: If a person's behavior is influenced by his/her conditions, then creating conditions of existence that are economically focused, and subsequently observing that his/her behavior is consistent with this context would not (scientifically) prove that the individual is economically driven.

S: What are you saying?

Q: Let us say I hypothesize that people are pain-avoiding and pleasure-seeking creatures. If,to prove my hypothesis, I set up the conditions such that people's options are limited to either choosing pleasure or pain in the next moment, then it would be a mistake for me to accept my hypothesis based on my observing that people choose the course of action that delivers pleasure over that which delivers pain in the moment. You see to a large extent that conditions shape the behavior, especially when the options offered are limited.

S: What are you suggesting? Are you saying that the Divine Plan is wrong?

Q: I'm suggesting that, given the adaptability of people, restricting choices consistent with the theory and proceeding as if the evidence proves the theory, is simply bad science.

I am also saying that people are capable of more than accumulating material wealth. Human behavior is not solely dictated by—or it can't be reduced to—the choice between seeking pleasure and avoiding pain in the moment.

S: What else is there? Even if what you say is true, the benefit of the theory to society is worth it. Look at the wealth humankind has amassed!

Q: Your question illustrates my point. Human beings are not limited to experiencing life as a competitive game in which the objective is to materially gain the most in each moment. Living life as a human is not limited to the choice between pain and pleasure.

Games offer a means of entertainment; with games we can choose to play them or not. Life is not a game.

S: I'm sorry, but I still don't see your point.

Q: I think this point will be clearer if we explore the essence of and potential in being human and the affect an egoistic economic system would have on people.

To Have More or to Be More

Q: Not unlike all other animals, we have an inherent biological striving for self-preservation and, consequently, we each must satisfy our need for food, water, sleep, protection/security, and reproduction. No doubt, the satisfaction of these needs constitutes a basic driving force in human behavior, in which the intensity of the striving for these needs is directly proportional to the degree to which they are unfulfilled.

S: It is just as I asserted, it is in our nature to be pain-avoiding and pleasure-seeking. It is pain of the unmet need (e.g., hunger) or the prospect for pleasure that directs our behavior.

Q: But our animal nature doesn't explain the whole story. We haven't the sufficient complex of instinctual behavioral patterns to direct behavior toward surviving in the environment. We do, however, have an intellectual capability that affords a great capacity for learning.

S: So intelligence makes up for the absence of instinctual regulation?

Q: Yes, our ability to adapt to whatever environment within which we find ourselves is largely dependent on our ability to learn.

S: Learning, then, is our means for preserving our existence?

Q: And if a person fails, refuses, or ceases to learn, then he/she becomes incapable of survival—unless of course another takes on that responsibility for him/her.

S: This makes sense especially when you consider at birth we are quite helpless for a considerable length of time—much more so than any other newborn creatures.

Q: Yes, humans are the most helpless of all animals in nature, for nature has not provided us with the instinctual traits necessary for self-reliance.

Hence, humans are born with an inherent desire to learn.

S: I can see how this makes sense: When I think about the very young I am reminded of their enormous hunger and thirst for learning.

Q: And the hunger and thirst for learning is not the same hunger and thirst that we have for food and water.
If learning is not experienced the body will not (necessarily) call out for it—we likely won't experience the pain/pleasure signal. The pleasure/pain dynamic does not have a primary role in this most important human need.

S: Then what is associated with this need?

Q: Again, if we turn our attention to the young child, what is commonly seen when a child learns something? What does the child visibly show he/she is experiencing?

S: Overall happiness, joy

Q: Yes, the child has an overall encompassing sense of joy—he/she just lights up!

S: And it is almost like he/she is in an altered state!

Q: Well, yes, the experience of joy is not so much a momentary pain/pleasure type sensation as it is a state of being.

S: What do you mean by "state of being"? Do you mean we become a different person?

Q: No, not a different person, but we are somehow transported to a different place; in this sense the process of learning is like a meditation —we become aware of or experience our human nature.

S: Are you saying through the process of learning we cease acting out of our animal nature?

Q: Yes, we cease being directed by circumstance and the habits of the past.

S: Can't animals learn?

Q: Animals can be trained. I can train my dog to respond in a particular way to a specific command or stimulus; but this is more about conditioning—behavior modification—than it is learning in the sense we have been discussing. Recognizing that animals react in response to the prospect of immediate pain or pleasure in the moment, we can teach animals to behave in a particular way using a stimulus–response process. In this sense we can say the dog has learned to follow commands.

S: So the notion that people living life by seeking pleasure or avoiding pain in the moment is descriptive of human beings acting out of their animal or lower nature?

Q: Yes; and where's the joy in that! Creating situations that would restrict or encourage people to do just this—to order their lives according to the pursuit of pleasure and the avoidance of pain—would limit human potential. It inhibits people from living according to their higher nature, from realizing their uniquely human potential. Learning in the sense that we are speaking about requires the ability to think about and beyond our thoughts; it requires a conscious awareness of our thinking process and the ability to go beyond a thought once held.

S: Is this related to Descartes' assertion: *I think, therefore I am?*

Q: Yes, what Descartes spoke to so concisely was humankind's ability to be consciously aware. The fact we are aware of our power to think is what makes us human and more than merely intelligent animals.

S: So the learning that we are discussing enables a future progressively different than the past?

Q: Yes, it makes it possible to live a life not determined by the past; a life not dictated by concretized notions or by instinctual-like habits of thought—we need not be prisoners of (our) thoughts.

S: I remember Descartes advanced the notion of questioning everything to find the truth.

Q: It is only through questions that we engage our process of thinking. Turning Descartes' famous phrase around we would say: *I am (human) therefore I (can) think . . . and I am aware of my thinking.*

We are unique in that we can be aware of our own awareness—we feel sad and are conscious of our sadness, we think and are conscious of our thoughts, we are bored and are conscious of our boredom, we are alive and are conscious of our aliveness. Being human means being consciously aware and ordering life according to this awareness.

S: So largely as a result of being aware of our awareness affords us (humankind) the ability to influence how life is lived; whereas all other animals are regulated in life by nature—instinctual regulation.

Q: Yes, although we are not instinctually regulated by nature we do live in and with nature and hence must comply with nature's laws. We aren't instinctually regulated but we rely heavily on nature—we are interdependent with nature.

S: But isn't it our choice to live as we so please?

Q: Yes, we do have a choice, but we also must live with the consequences of our choices.

Nature can't be altered or controlled without exacting potentially devastating effects. If we choose to ignore or not awaken to our interdependence with nature, then we will destroy ourselves—it is called committing suicide by nature.

S: So nature provides all other animals their reality and we participate with nature to create our reality.

Q: Yes, in so doing we influence or create the reality of all other animals as well.

S: It is quite a responsibility that we have!

Q: That is for sure! After all we are create-ures, and we create our reality.

This choice of living life as we see fit not only includes the choices we make relative to how our relationship with nature is lived, but also the choices we make relative to being in accord with our own nature.

S: I am not quite clear on what you are getting at.

Q: Well, we can choose to structure life—bringing (our sense of) order to life—by seeking to satisfy the desires emerging out of our animal nature or by appealing to our higher, uniquely human nature.

S: Are you saying we can either act like animals or we can act like people; that we can be barbarians or we can be civilized?

Q: Not exactly, although I suspect we've all met some animals that have acted far more civilized than some people we know.

What I am saying is that we can choose to focus attention on our lower level desires as a way of ordering our world or we can choose to appeal to our higher level nature. We can create societal systems that either cause individuals to structure their lives consistent with the needs and wants we share with all other animals or that cause individuals to orient their lives consistent with realizing higher level capabilities that only human beings have.

Recall that we discussed earlier that if we set up the conditions such that people's options are limited to choosing between pleasure and pain in the next moment, then it would be a mistake to conclude that the primary driver in people's behavior is pleasure-seeking and pain-avoiding—these are lower level behavioral drivers we share with all other animals.

S: So, if we order life according to the notion that people are pleasure-seeking and pain-avoiding, then are we guiding people to order life according to their animal nature?

Q: Yes, and as a result we are limiting the human potential that lies in every person. It causes individuals not to recognize the value of being human; often times this awakening is only realized when a person faces the prospect of his/her life coming to an end.

S: So we are more than intelligent animals capable of ordering life according to the satisfaction of selfish passions in the moment?

Q: Yes, life need not be structured according to this very limited view of what it means to be human.

We share with all other animals the ability to know the world through the five senses; and yet, unlike all other animals, we have the ability to transcend the current circumstance in which we find ourselves. We are able to perceive and think beyond the moment—with the arrow of time pointed forward and/or backward—this affords us the capability of producing knowledge—this means we can discover and also create theory.

S: So, by employing hindsight and/or foresight, our future need not be a replay of the patterns of the past.

Q: Yes, as long as our sense of order is congruent with our higher nature and informs the world-space (context) we create.

S: What you are saying is that our sense of order in effect creates the context in which we live—we talked about this previously.

Q: Acting as human beings enables us to become (more) human: Creating a human world enables each individual living in that world to become (more) human.

S: But aren't we already human? How can we become what we already are?

Q: Animals can't become human, only humans can. My dog at birth is as much of a dog as she will ever be. At birth animals have all the abilities, all the understanding they could ever have. We can't say the same thing about a human being. All qualities or dimensions of humankind are there, potentially, for future development through the act of living.

S: What are examples of the dimensions for development you refer to?

Q: There are many, but a few you might recognize include social development, moral development, and development of self.

S: I can understand social and moral development, but I am not quite clear what is meant by development of self.

Q: Development of self—which flows from the fact we are consciously aware of our awareness—involves to a large extent the development of a deeper understanding of who or what we (as humans) are; the development of a self-concept.

S: What does a deeper understanding of ones' self mean and why is it so important?

Q: I suspect the answer to any one of the two questions you pose will also inform the answer to the other.

Understanding ones' self begins with the determination of who you are. So, I ask, who are you?

S: I am Adam Smith. I am the author of *The Wealth of Nations.*

Q: These are all facts about you; they inform me of what you are called (your name) and the title of a book you have written (an accomplishment). What these suggest is that your sense of self is one that is referenced to the objects or products in your life. Your understanding of self is determined by objects/things "out there" with which you associate your self. It is an external reference that makes the concept of self quite precarious.

S: Precarious?

Q: In identifying self in terms of externalities— attaching to the temporal things in life necessarily means that "who we are"— our sense of self—changes as circumstances change. Take away one of these attachments and the sense of self will likely diminish.

S: So we rise and fall as circumstances rise and fall!

Q: As beliefs, ideas, notions, titles, positions, and outcomes that we attach the self to and define the self by rise and fall, then so too does our self-concept. Consequently, with this level of understanding of self individuals are very likely to defend those things that they define themselves by in order to remain who they (believe they) are. If I am defined by what I attach to "me"—the things that are mine—then if they are threatened, then necessarily it is a threat to "me." We see the threat as an attempt to makes less of "me."

This stage is egocentric wherein the focus of attention is on "me" and what is mine; and the more I have means the more I am—it is all about "me." This "me"—who I believe I am—is nothing but a collection of things and becoming more of a person translates into having more things (e.g., more money, more cars, grander title, bigger house, bigger image)—we become the things (we consume) in life. Hence, the common phrase descriptive of an egocentered individual: *he/she is full of him/herself.*

S: Don't accomplishments, possessions, positions, and so on, provide us with a favorable (self) image especially in the eyes of others? It seems to me that this is related to my notion of fellow-feeling.

Q: Yes, in a way it is, because our self-concept would be dependent on what we believe others think about us, the image they have of us. But again, this is just defining ones' self based on externalities.

S: But "fellow-feeling" is very real: We all experience it!

Q: That is true, but we should not define the self by it. Whether you have a favorable public image or not, should not determine who you are on the inside. Image after all is at base imaginary.

S: Who you are on the inside? I am not sure I understand what you are saying.

Q: If your concept of self is dependent on the objects and things "out there"—such as the opinion of others—that you attach to and define your self by, then your sense of who you are is based on what has taken form in time—a material orientation or referencing—which is always subject to change.

S: So you are saying, if who I am is what I have and given that what I have can be taken away or lost in time, then my sense of who I am is subject to change.

Q: Yes, and if these are taken away or diminished then so too is ones' self-concept. With a sense of who we are resting on time-bound things, it is understandable why individuals become protective of them.

Stripping all these things away, we see that what is not dependent on circumstances is conscious awareness; this conscious awareness is always present.

S: Conscious awareness?

Q: As we've discussed, human beings are not only intelligent, human beings are also quite consciously aware and it is this latter dimension that is uniquely human.

       We are aware of our position in this or that organization but we aren't the position. We are aware of how we feel about this or that but we aren't our feelings. We are aware of the thoughts we have but we aren't our thoughts. We are aware of what we do and what we have but we are not what we do or what we have. We are not these things, but we are aware of all these things.

S: So this self that I am is an aware consciousness?

Q: Yes.

S: Then how or where does the notion of self-development fit in? If we are conscious awareness, then what is there to develop?

Q: What develops is our understanding of self (and correlatively our place in the world)—we deepen our awareness. Because we are aware of our awareness we must order (bring order to and make meaning of) our world, which necessarily means developing a sense of who we are and how we fit in.

S: This seems similar to Protagoras's assertion that *man is the measure of all things.*

Q: What we are saying is that meaning is a human invention: Knowing that we exist—conscious awareness again—we must make sense of our world and of our existence in it.

S: So reality—our reality—is not independent of us?

Q: We participate in creating the reality we experience; more specifically the things in our experience do not come to us prelabeled or preordered; they don't come with little tags attached identifying and describing their meaning—we are the measure of all things.

       Unlike animals who rely on instinctual regulation and who have experience and simply react in the moment to this experience, human beings are not similarly regulated and cannot rely on nature to order their experiences in the world. Human beings (must) make meaning of it all. We bring order to the world in light of our purposes, which are socially mediated.

S: Including our sense of self?

Q: Yes, and hence the development of an understanding and sense of self is influenced by the social system within which we live.

S: I understand what you are saying but I am still finding it difficult to see how this sense of self develops.

Q: Unlike physical development that involves outward material growth, the development of self is interior development in which an individual gains an increasingly deeper (internal) awareness of self.

S: So through development individuals become more self-absorbed?

Q: On the contrary, by gaining a deeper awareness of the interior self, a person becomes increasingly less ego-centered, less materially oriented or attached—material objects are commonly used to define "me," the objective material self. As a result an individual is able to know his/her self as a subject and not an object; a person is able to see that he/she, while being a separate self—like every other individual person—is also at the same time deeply connected to each and every other self.

S: If who we are is not dependent on the circumstances we find our self in, then how can you also say that our sense of self is socially mediated?

Q: I understand the confusion: We are conscious awareness and this doesn't depend on circumstances; but the likelihood of us coming to this realization—the process of our development—is influenced by the collective mindset of the society we live in.

S: Our society is our teacher?

Q: That's a different way of stating it and I believe it captures the idea.

In fact I think we can say that society can only teach what it knows and going beyond what society knows requires considerable (individual) commitment to overcome the pressure to conform to society's way of being.

S: So we are both helped and hindered by society in our development?

Q: It is probably not so much hindered as it is not helped. Individual development happens a lot easier than societal development. It takes a lot of individuals to advance a society in its development.

S: Let's briefly get back to development of self. In general what are the stages of development?

Q: In general self-development is about interior development, going inward, which results in greater depth of self. Another way of thinking about the development of self is to view it as the development of self-identity—what we identify with in establishing our self-concept. We can either reference the self externally or internally, with the latter corresponding to greater depth.

S: The more externally referenced a person is, the less developed is his/her self identity.

Q: And the more superficial and self-absorbed, the more ego-centered he/she is. Identifying the self with surface-level material things—maintaining an objective self—keeps one feeling the need to defend and protect that which you identify with (e.g., ideas, possessions, position, etc.).

However, by going inward, by gaining a deeper sense of self, one can gain a broader (as well as a deeper) understanding of self—a person is able to identify less with things and more with the essence of his/her humanness—which is shared with other individuals.

S: I get the difference between an externally referenced self and an internally referenced self. However, I am not clear on the notion of a broader self-identity.

Q: As we move deeper into the self we are able to identify with an increasing number of other selves as a result of an increasing awareness that this individual "I/me" who I think I am, is inextricably connected to a "we." We become less of an isolated or separate self and more connected to other selves because we increasingly acknowledge a commonality.

S: Might it be something like the separate self-identity is somewhat less than a self identifying with a group of other selves, such as family?

Q: Yes, and as we increase the group definition that defines the "we" from say family to ethnicity, then our identity would have greater breadth—we move from a small sense of self to a larger sense or identity of self when we move from being egocentric to ethnocentric.

S: And if we identify self with the society within which we live, then we'd have a sociocentric concept of self.

Q: Yes. For example, this is where an individual identifying him/her self with being an American would have the effect of him/her relating to, empathizing with, and caring about other Americans like him/her—but not the Russians. So harming another American—one of us—is like harming me, but harming the Russians does not affect me or us; therefore, it doesn't result in the same feeling and conclusion.

S: I can see where the sense of self, the self we identify with, becomes increasingly larger **(from self to self to self to self, etc.)** as we gain a deeper understanding by turning the focus of our awareness inward.

Q: We gain a far deeper and broader understanding of who we are. Accordingly, we come to realize a diminution of "me" and a deeper connection between "I" and "we" — in which the "we" is increasingly inclusive, eventually comprising not only human beings, but all sentient beings.

S: So over all, where are we as a society as we begin the 21st century in America?

Q: Because, in our society, we've lost touch with the unifying force that is the essence of our being, all we have are I's putting "Me" (and "Us") first. We are stuck at the lower stages of development—intelligent animals absent of a greater sense of self (and meaning).

S: Why are we stuck?

Q: Recall we briefly discussed the influence of society? That is, because our society directs each of its members to maximize his/her (material) self-interest, it unavoidably encourages an egoic concern for self in the name of wealth accumulation. As a consequence of this pursuit of self–interest, most individuals are externally referenced and identify the self with the objective "me."

S: How is this keeping us stuck?

Q: Since there is no natural satiation point for the objects of our desire, we are forever on the treadmill running to consume more for the sake of "me." The egocentered self tends to focus attention on what has been and what can be consumed—I am more the more I have, might be the mantra.

More to the point, this selfish passion—putting "me" above "I"—is irrational. The continuous pursuit of material wealth is inconsistent with self-development and is therefore not in proportion to the development of this "I" that we each are and must become. Individuals strive throughout life to have more and pay little to no attention to becoming more—the having way of life supplants being in life.

A Likely Development

The purpose of this discussion is to bring to light the relationship between the precepts underlying economic thought and the traditional design and management of our business organizations.

Q: Let's begin at the very beginning: How does a business begin?

S: It begins with an idea; an idea to provide a product or service that meets a need.

Q: So, all that is needed for a business is an idea that meets a need?

S: Well, the idea cannot materialize into a business without capital. Capital is not only required to pay labor and to produce the product or service, it is also needed to promote and distribute the product.

Q: Yes, capital is critical to a business, but we mustn't forget the idea is the essence of a business.

S: Of course, the idea is the seed from which a business enterprise grows and capital is what makes it grow; capital is also the measure of its growth.

Q: But capital alone is not enough! Developing a business is difficult; it takes tremendous commitment to create a viable business and this commitment comes from believing in—having faith in and commitment to—the idea.

S: So if those with the business idea are able to secure the requisite capital and find within themselves the courage and commitment to venture into unknown territory, they can transform their idea into an enterprise that produces a product or service that returns a profit.

Q: This diagram clearly shows how providing a product or service that satisfies the needs of people will begin to turn the business cycle. As the product or service meets the needs of people, market share and corresponding revenue are returned to the producer and with a

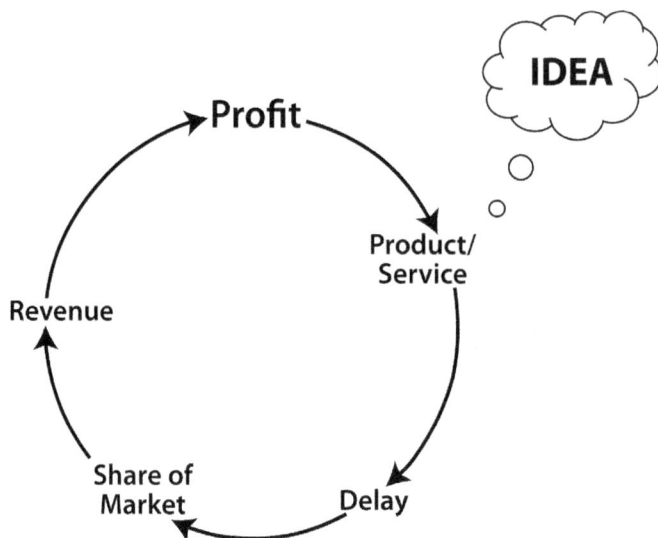

Self-reinforcing Business Cycle

Figure 1   Self-reinforcing business cycle.

reasonable profit derived from the revenue gained, the business can be self-supporting.

S: Once the cycles begins turning it will likely continue to turn.

Q: If things don't change, then yes. If things change, then all bets are off.

S: What could possibly change?

Q: There are a number of things that could change: the market dynamics could change, the owners of the business and/or those in authority could lose focus.

S: Of course I understand if other organizations enter the market offering competitive products or services, and/or if customers' needs or expectations change, then the market for the idea may no longer be what it was and so the original thinking around the idea may have to change.

Q: What I think you are saying is, those with authority over the business need to be flexible and adaptive for the business to establish and maintain a share of market to keep the cycle turning.

S: Yes, the wise business manager must always be willing to test theory against practice! But this does not mean there is a loss of focus.

Q: Well, according to one of the key precepts of economic theory— maximize self-interest— as the business cycle continues to turn the owner/partners of the organization (or their professional management surrogates) are compelled to grow the business and return greater profits in the next quarter and in the next year—the financial performance of the organization can become paramount.

S: If the business is prospering, then the idea has provided evidence of its potential for financial gain. I don't quite understand where and how commitment is lost.

Q: Let's redraw the diagram to reflect what we are saying. Feeling compelled to grow the business and return greater profit, the purpose of the business tacitly shifts from satisfying peoples' needs to producing profit. Essentially, providing a product and/or service becomes a means to the overarching objective of greater profit, of unlimited material growth of the organization.

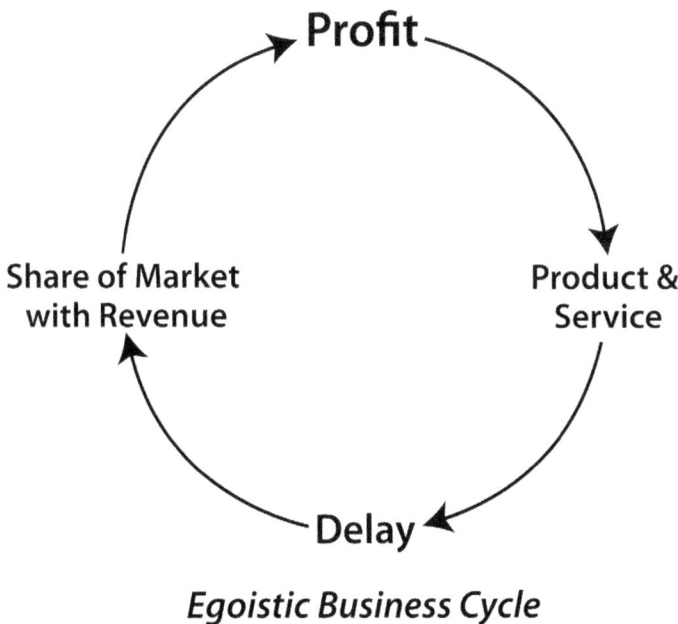

Profit

Product & Service

Delay

Share of Market with Revenue

Egoistic Business Cycle

Figure 2   Egoistic business cycle.

S: The conduct of business is to add to the material wealth: Of course, the business of business is profit!

Q: Wait: Step back and think what your statement implies. What once was the essence of the business—an idea for a product or service intended to satisfy peoples' needs—now becomes secondary and the focus of those in authority turns to the organization's financial goals and away from meeting people's needs. The product or service becomes a cost to the business of making a profit.

It should be understandable why many organizations find it necessary to reintroduce themselves to the customer—unfortunately, solely for reasons of profit.

S: What do you mean "unfortunately"?

Q: The compulsion for greater and greater profit will likely have an adverse effect on those employed, as well as on the organization itself and those it serves.

Let us explore what else is usually associated with the emergence of the need to employ the services of others to carry out the daily business operations so as to satisfactorily meet the growing demand.

S: I can see where it can become a bit more complex because one not only must manage the business but now also manage those doing the work of the business.

I see the solution to this as being to break the organization up into smaller pieces. That is, partition it into more manageable parts, in which each part is viewed and managed as a separate component.

Q: How do you suggest this is done?

S: The partitioning would occur in functional areas—those with the same or very similar tasks to perform would form a department that can be managed.

Q: With each piece being managed, just how is the business managed?

S: A chain of command is employed to control the various pieces, usually referred to as departments or functional areas. Structurally, the organization is hierarchically configured with the central locus of control at the top. That is, each is answerable or accountable to the next higher level within the organization.

Q: So the next higher level does what for the next lower level?

S: Planning and directing the work.

Q: Then direction and information flows downward through the hierarchy. This seems to imply that the thinking is done at the top and doing occurs at the bottom of the hierarchy?

S: Yes, think of the top of the hierarchy as the head and the bottom as the body.

Q: And the head controls the movement of the body. Just how is this done?

S: Those at the top— management— set numerical goals for the organization and cascade these or related goals down through the chain of command to each functional component, associating the attainment of each goal with a promise of reward or a threat of punishment.

In other words, management directs the behavior of employees by aligning their objectives with those of the organization, thus causing people to continually strive to satisfy the organization's objectives by attaching the satisfaction of their needs to the achievement of the organization's goals.

Q: The satisfaction of an employee's needs is conditioned on him/her making a positive contribution to the organization's profit goal.

S: Yes. If the goals are met or exceeded, then people are commensurately rewarded.

Q: So it is an economic arrangement or contract between the organization and the employee?

S: Yes, logically you pay for the performance you get.

Q: What if an employee's performance is dependent on the performance of others in the organization: How does management know what's what? How is an individual's contribution isolated and known separated from the effects of others?

S: As I stated, each department, each employee has an objective—a numerical goal—against which each department or individual is measured. Management has the numbers!

Q: [Even though you can point to separate numbers doesn't mean that meeting these can be independently accomplished. I suspect the logic you are using is really a logical fallacy; but we will explore this a bit later, so let's just continue.]

So by playing on the pain–pleasure dynamic, people are tacitly taught the *rules of business* and in the process acquire the habits of behavior to not only meet their subsistence needs, but also to continually strive to want and have more; and in so doing attain a greater sense of esteem. In essence people are guided in developing their sense of self in a particular way consistent with the rules of business.

S: Yes, this is how those at the top of the organization direct the behavior of those at the bottom to accomplish the organization's goal.

Q: So they direct by setting goals, but do they also prescribe how the goals are to be accomplished?

S: Not necessarily: With results being all that matters, generally skilled labor can use any means. With this mechanism the organization runs like a *well-oiled* machine toward accomplishing its profit objective.

Q: I can see that through this quantitative and materialistic approach meeting organizational objectives simply becomes a means of creating and satisfying wants; and so for those in power, the engine of unlimited growth is set in motion.

S: Yes, the industriousness of labor is assured.

Q: Then the achievement of desired results is assured with the plans and goals provided by management.

S: It is not that automatic: Management must also administer over the performance of departments and individuals to ensure goals are attained.

Q: Okay, how is this done?

S: Each and every activity is associated with a number that reflects the activity's contribution to profit. In effect, everybody is assessed in regard to his/her contribution to the organization's profit objective.

Q: So managing a business becomes a numerical skill-based activity, with knowledge of the business operation being synonymous with knowledge of the numbers?

S: What counts is what can be counted: So the focus of management naturally is what is measurable and quantifiable.

Q: So, with a clear number in mind, management can readily assess the acceptability of an individual or activity?

S: Yes, and with everyone's performance measured relative to his/her contribution to the organization's numerical goals, everyone can be rated, ranked, and judged.

Q: And correspondingly labeled? Are you saying that management identifies and rewards the *good* performers and singles out the *not-so-good* or *poor* performers for corrective action?

S: Yes, and labeling also addresses or speaks to my notion of fellow-feeling. In addition to being paid for performance, everyone wants to be thought of as valued and successful—especially by others—thus, everyone is enticed to vie for *good-performer* status.

Also for management to maintain control, any resource or activity that does not contribute to profit loses its value to the organization and, therefore, theses exceptions must be dealt with: People must experience the consequences of their poor performance.

Q: This appears to be quite a scientific and somewhat mechanical view of things—it sounds like it is designed to run like clockwork! I suppose following this theory no organization could fail to attain what was desired.

S: Actually business organizations do fail.

Q: If something is controlled, then how does it fail—unless of course it is controlled to fail?

It seems that the approach doesn't really provide control but rather only the illusion of control!

I ask you to reflect on our earlier discussion about being human. What if people can't be managed as if they were objects without at the same time inhibiting development and causing destruction to the self? What if those employed are not objects but subjects?

Doesn't this approach to business expunge all meaning from human life, defining its worth strictly in monetary terms? Doesn't this approach to structuring and managing a business organization assume that people have no inherent motivation, no will—that they are intelligent animals who can be trained to do as desired? Isn't this clearly incongruent with our previous discussion on the human condition?

With the employment of others there are now many individuals who need to know how and where to apply their knowledge and skills in support of the business, so I can understand the need to bring order to create proper conditions for effective and meaningful work. The aim should be to coordinate and harmonize the efforts of many. Why wouldn't treating people as subjects and not objects likely prove to be far more productive in this regard?

Managing Results Through Selfish Passions

THE CAPITALISTIC PRINCIPLE THAT EACH ONE SEEKS HIS OWN
PROFIT AND THUS CONTRIBUTES TO THE HAPPINESS OF ALL
BECOMES THE GUIDING PRINCIPLE OF HUMAN BEHAVIOR.

—ERICH FROMM

The purpose of this discussion is to explore the effect that the compulsion for material self-interest, profit maximization could possibly have on those employed by the organization, and by extension, on society.

Q: As we previously discussed, creating conditions that direct people to focus on maximizing their material self-interest unavoidably encourages an egocentered sense of self, which tends to focus attention on what has been and can be consumed—creating the belief that *I am more the more I have*.

S: But management must direct the efforts of those employed in support of the business' productivity/profit goal. Hence, appealing to people's material self-interest as a management principle would no doubt contribute to the industriousness of labor and, correspondingly, to the productivity of the enterprise and, in turn, to the wealth of society.

Q: Perhaps. But it would depend on the business condition as well as how you define productivity and what you are really seeking to do—what you truly care about.

S: Just what condition would inhibit the effectiveness of appealing to selfish passion from yielding greater productivity? It seems that it is a logical connection, no matter the circumstance. And what do you mean by *what you care about*? Isn't it obviously the growth of profit!

Q: First, let us address the issue of circumstance wherein appealing to the selfish passion of employees and yet not being able to adequately satisfy their material interest would not sustain their industriousness. In other words, when the answer to *what's in it for me* no longer satisfies, then the lever *if you do that, then you will get this* will no longer move another in the desired direction.

S: Isn't their desire to satisfy their wants still compelling?

Q: Yes it is; especially within Western society.

S: Therefore, I would think that leveraging this desire would promote people's productivity, if not increase it.

Q: What is tacitly learned in the use of such a lever is that the job/activity has no value apart from the material gain it returns—you see, in this system, employees are conditioned to manage by results as well.

Hence if the scarcity turns real, then the value of the result of performing the activity can't satisfy the desired gain—there is no motivation for goal-directed behavior!

S: What do you mean, scarcity turns real?

Q: You see, the statement *if you do that, then you will get this* creates a condition of artificial scarcity. It is not that management in authority doesn't have something desirable, it's that management is making the getting of what is wanted conditional on the results that come from the activity; they are creating an artificial scarcity to incite others to act.

Now when scarcity is real, when there isn't enough to satisfy everyone, then management gets more than they bargained for.

S: More than they bargained for? Please explain what you mean.

Q: In abundant times, there is plenty to go around so the management–worker contract *if you do that, then you will get this* incites a feeding frenzy among employees. The result is everyone is doing as the organization desires and getting what is desired (by them). But when scarcity turns real, then not everyone gets what he/she desires and not everyone is doing what is desired.

S: Not everyone doing as desired? If you mean they aren't working as hard, then I would argue that such conditions would make people work even harder to get what they want.

Q: Yes, it makes them strive harder; however, not to accomplish the organization's goal but to accomplish their goal. To this end looking good serves the same purpose as doing well.

S: But the contract *if you do that, then you will get this* says they only get what they want if the organization gets what it wants.

Q: Remember the organization's goal is only important to them to the extent that it returns what they want; and with numerical results being the thing, rigging the system and fudging the numbers become distinct options.

S: Are you saying that all that matters is the result?

Q: Yes, and they've learned this lesson from the organization. If it is okay for the organization to focus on results, then why shouldn't the worker do the same!

Given this dynamic, when artificial scarcity turns real, the materialistic-based management methods that appeared to be effective in abundant times will no longer be so—they will reach their limit.

S: What do you mean by *reach their limit*?

Q: The area of opportunity to satisfy needs and wants diminishes, it becomes harder and harder for everyone to satisfy his/her material self-interests and realize the promise of ever-increasing material gain.

S: I can see if things are not abundant, then there is less to go around.

Q: Less going around means less coming around. Moreover, given the insatiability of material wants, satisfaction is never realized once and for all; hence the breakdown of the system would be much more apparent in times of scarcity. So, not only can fewer and fewer receive positive reinforcement, the promise of ever-increasing material gain will go unmet.

In other words, as abundance turns to scarcity, meeting profit goals becomes more difficult with fewer and fewer experiencing the promise and pleasure of material gain.

S: And the number experiencing negative consequences increases?

Q: Yes, and their commitment and effort will likely be adjusted downward to match the return; while at the same time those in authority positions will tend to ensure their material interests are served.

S: So it is not favorable economic exchanges that are not taking place, it just that they are taking place only among a few. Now a statement you made much earlier in our conversation—*trickle down doesn't*—is making much more sense to me.

Q: When scarcity is real, then self-interested behavior turns back onto itself, cutting off its invisible (helping) hands, where only those in authority realize gain.

In fact the errors in assumptions of both neoclassical economics and its associated management system are fully exposed when limits to economic growth materialize.

S: What do you mean *errors in assumptions* in economic theory? Just what errors are you referring to?

Q: This relates to the second issue, that is, what we mean by productivity and what we are really seeking to do; which is directly influenced by what is assumed and believed about the nature of humankind.

S: Can you expand on this a bit? Please explain.

Q: Well, if you assume humankind is at base pleasure-seeking, driven primarily, if not solely, by material self-interest, then, logically, what you would seek to do in business would be consistent with this belief.

S: Isn't producing greater and greater material wealth doing just that?

Q: Yes, it is.

S: Well, then, I don't see what the issue is.

Q: On the other hand, if you believe people are not at base pleasure-seeking and driven by selfish passion, then what you would seek to do in business would be entirely different.

You see if you proceed on the wrong assumption, then you would adversely impact human development.

S: These adverse effects you speak of, what are they?

Q: What I am speaking about is the basis on which the entire theory rests; that is, the premise that people are primarily selfishly motivated by material gain—recall previously that we discussed what it means to be human. Given this understanding, not only does incentive-based management theory break down in times of real scarcity, but the neoclassical (egoistic) economic theory adversely impacts the development of self. If I may quote Gregory Bateson from *Steps to an Ecology of Mind*:

> A screwdriver is not seriously affected when, in an emergency, we use it as a wedge; and a hammer's outlook on life is not affected because we sometimes use its handle as a simple lever. But in social manipulation our tools are people, and people learn and they acquire habits which are more subtle and pervasive than the tricks which the blueprinter teaches them. (1972, p. 163)

S: Yes, I understand. But aren't we simply appealing to people's natural desires? People aren't being used for something that the Designer did not intend! If its part of the Divine Plan, then it can't be manipulation; it's not against people's will.

Q: Your question and assertions presuppose the validity of the very belief that is in question.

Perhaps it would be helpful if we briefly explored the influence of the economic system on society; after all, people sustain their existence and a way of being through the societal institutions that they create.

Egoistic Economics in Western Society

[I}T WILL BE SUFFICIENT TO JUSTIFY THE REJECTION OF THE WHOLE IF I SHALL FIND IN EACH SOME GROUND FOR DOUBT . . . THE REMOVAL FROM BELOW OF THE FOUNDATION NECESSARILY INVOLVES THE DOWNFALL OF THE WHOLE EDIFICE.

— Rene Descartes

Q: Within a society a reinforcing cycle exists whereby the social system mediates the development of a particular trait and, in turn, the system is favorably selective of those who exhibit the behavior reflective of that trait.

S: So you are saying that a society favors those individuals whose traits best align with its values and beliefs! What might this general character profile be in Western society?

Q: Yes, and based on my observations I'd say most people believe themselves to be independent beings who are unashamedly competitive, with a desire to amass great wealth.

S: So words such as "individualistic," "competitive," "materialistic," "self-interested" would be descriptive of those societal traits?

Q: Yes, I'd say so. Interestingly, these traits are consistent with the tenets of the system of political economy you put forth in the *Wealth of Nations.*

S: Well, of course: My work was grounded in the belief that people are motivated by materially centered selfish passions—my first maxim is that people naturally seek to further their material self-interests.

Q: And the theory also assumes we each are independent beings so the wealth of society is the linear sum of the wealth acquired by each of its independent members.

S: Yes, the greatest good is served as each seeks to maximize his/her material self-interest.

Q: Doesn't this then lead us to the second maxim in your theory, that of unlimited growth?

S: If we consider that nature holds more than what an individual could possibly acquire, our potential for the accumulation of material wealth is without bound.

Q: So, according to this system, we must be driven to accumulate greater and greater levels of wealth. Hence the focus on and commitment to increasing economic growth.

S: Yes, it goes without saying that the wealth inherent in nature is ours to have and to do with according to our desires. With dominion over nature we are free to do with it as we see fit as long as it is good for the economy—as long as our actions add to the sum total of material wealth of society.

Q: Things are *going well* as long as the economy is growing?

S: Well, yes, isn't the economy the source of the satisfaction of our self-interest and the improvement of our lot?

Q: I agree that a society needs a strong economy.

S: And people should be good to the economy!

Q: You seem to be implying that if we are good to the economy, it will be good to us.

S: A society's success is dependent on the strength of its economy, is it not?

Q: Yes, of course there is interdependence between the viability of society and its economy: A strong economy provides the means of survival in life. So from this perspective we don't serve the economy, the economy serves us—it must meet our needs.

S: A society needs a strong economy; one that amasses wealth and continually grows.

   Hence to keep the economy strong consumption of goods and services must correspondingly increase!

Q: Let's rethink this: Feeding the economy and feeding humankind are related but not identical; moreover, developing an insatiable need to consume results in an unsustainable society.

S: What do you mean unsustainable? Please explain.

Q: The satisfaction of an insatiable and unceasing need to consume requires unbounded resources—something this earth does not have.

S: But the resources in nature are renewable and therefore are they not limitless?

Q: Yes, nature renews itself, but at a rate far less than is required to support the rate of unfettered consumption.

S: Unfettered consumption? Isn't the economy simply meeting the needs of society?

Q: It seems there is confusion about what the needs of people are and what the needs of an economic system with the aim of unlimited material growth are—let's be clear with our language. Peoples' self-preservation needs for food, shelter, and clothing are physiologically regulated, which means there is a point at which the (inherent) desire to fulfill the need ceases—needs-based consumption is not insatiable.

If the economic system's aim is to grow without bound, then this ever upwardly spiraling production/consumption cycle cannot be supported by consumption solely based on inherent human need.

S: So what are you saying?

Q: Well, if the economy is to function consistent with its two primary maxims—maximize material self-interest and unlimited material growth—then, as you previously stated, consumption must correspondingly increase without bound. Therefore, the system must change to align with the nature of humankind or there must be a shift (within people) from inherent *human-need* consumption, which is bounded, to *ego-want* consumption, which is insatiable.

S: Isn't self-interest the driving force in the economy? Why do you say there must be a shift to ego-want consumption?

Q: As long as the self identifies with the objective "me" then yes, self-interest can support unlimited growth; but if the self-identity corresponds to a more developed sense of self, the increasingly integrative "I"—as we previously discussed—then this integral self doesn't align with material self-interest and unlimited material growth. We don't inherently or necessarily need more and more, but the egocentric person surely wants more and more—the ego can never have too much. In this way the egoic self becomes the requisite underlying force supporting—the engine that produces—unlimited growth.

S: I believe there is some misunderstanding: The aim of the capitalistic economic system is to accumulate and amass material wealth in society. Instead you have made it sound as though the economic system is itself self-serving.

Q: Yes, that is what I am saying.

Let's look at the dynamics: Unlimited production and material growth require unlimited consumption; and unlimited consumption will not be realized if the drive to consume is based on satiable needs. So allow me to rephrase your statement: The aim of the egoistic economic system is to accumulate material wealth with the ego's insatiable need to consume being the means to this end. A tactic commonly used by the U.S. government to stimulate a slow economy is to provide a tax rebate to people with the explicit associated wish that individuals will in turn spend and consume, thus feeding the economy.

S: And if the economy gets stronger, then society becomes wealthier and the greater good is served!

Q: Let's see who is served in this system. In the United States just under 85% of the total net worth is held by 20% of the people; or 80% of the people lay claim to just over 15% of the total net worth in society. So wealth is highly concentrated among a relatively small percentage of the people in society.

S: But as those 80% strive to improve their lot then the industriousness of society is assured.

Q: And the top 20% are better served as a result! In effect 80% of society serves the economic system and 20% are well served by the system. So rather than having a system that is in service to society, we have society serving the system and serving those with the power to change the system.

A system in support of self-interest will unavoidably become self-serving. If the system's mantra is "maximize your (material) self interest," then why wouldn't those in authority engage the system and seek to perpetuate it to their advantage?

Let's look at what else is happening while the wealthy get wealthier. As egocentrism becomes dominant then self-development becomes dormant; the majority of individuals in society get stuck at egocentric and ethnocentric stages—there might be material growth but little development of self is realized.

A Challenge to Tradition

Usually when people think, they always consider
themselves right;
but when they put it into practice,
what they thought was right may turn out to
be wrong.
This is wherein folly and wisdom differ.

—The Masters of Huainan

S: Well, you make it sound like a devious plot, when in fact it is all part of the Divine Plan.

Q: Devious! I don't mean to imply that the intention of those who crafted the system was not honorable. What I do mean to communicate is that the theory is grounded in misunderstanding and error—especially given what is known about humankind today.

If you are a good hard worker, if you go along with what the market expects, then the theory leads you to believe you will acquire wealth, position, and power; it's all part of the Divine Plan. This is an alluring promise. But even you've acknowledged that rarely will everyone realize the promise—and the statistics on the distribution of net worth and income bear this out.

It's deception if and only if we acknowledge it and yet continue to promote the promise!

S: How could it be in error when, as was stated in *The Wealth of Nations*, it is part of God's plan!

Q: The source of the economic theory we've been adhering to is not Divine—as you had suggested—by any stretch of the imagination. Time has provided the proof of this! The invisible hand does not adequately regulate the system—the market is not self-correcting. Why else would we require additional mechanisms (e.g., the chief of the federal bank increasing/decreasing interest rates; or government bailouts and stimulus packages) to tinker with things?

S: OK, but haven't we realized tremendous wealth! After all it does work!

Q: Yes it works, but for only a few. If you focus only with one eye open—on the material aspects of life and societal wealth accumulation—then I can see why you could draw this conclusion. We must not forget that although some have realized great personal wealth, many more have not. Also, the improved distribution of material wealth was precipitated by both the creation of labor unions and the enactment of legislation, in the early 1900s, that forced and enforced a more just distribution, not to mention safer working conditions. Yet, today, as we've previously discussed, the distribution is far from optimal with the top 20% of the population owning the vast majority (84%) of the wealth in society. It's working, but for whom?

S: If this is against our nature, if it is as detrimental as you make it sound, then how could people allow this to happen for so many years? It must be part of our nature!

Q: People's conformance to its requirements can't be used as proof of its alignment with human nature. As previously discussed, it is both deceptive and inappropriate to limit people to functioning within a context and then conclude, by observing that the behavior conforms with that context, that the context is in harmony with how people really are. Remember, people are adaptable to the conditions within which they must live.

S: So what are you suggesting?

Q: People within this society have dynamically adapted to the requirements of egoistic capitalism by developing character traits that enable them to cooperate with and succeed in the system. We've identified these traits earlier in our discussion—recall individualistic, competitive, materialistic, self-interested.

Further, as we've just discussed, the pursuit of unlimited material growth uses people; it doesn't serve people.

S: Again, I believe you are misunderstanding. The economic theory advances the individual–it supports those who seek to get things out of life.

Q: Yes, but it's the same stuff for everyone, material wealth!

S: What is wrong with that! Just look at the number of people who have gained from this system!

Q: Through the system of egoistic capitalism success in life is defined by the things one can accumulate; a full life is a life filled with things. And further—adding insult to injury—most everyone will not realize it. Its purpose doesn't serve the development of the person, but rather only the amassing of material wealth, and with a very unbalanced societal distribution.

On the surface it seems to advance individualism, but in reality it requires conformity–each and every individual is expected to be the same and to have the same goal for his/her life.

S: So exactly with what are you taking issue?

Q: I am not questioning that over the years economics has improved its mathematical rigor. It has both developed and honed its models, but it hasn't fostered a type of learning that involves challenging the continued validity of its own underlying assumptions. Even though our knowledge of humankind has increased, our economics has remained stuck to an outdated theory of human nature. The science of humankind has evolved, but our economics—which rests squarely on an understanding of the theory of humankind—has not, correspondingly, evolved. Economics has been increasing its precision, while ignoring its accuracy—it is precise in missing the target.

If economics is indeed a science—and not a religion—then it is imperative that we rethink it with our current understanding of humankind.

Vision of a New Order:
Rethinking the Economy's Precepts

[I]T IS POSSIBLE TO SAY THAT NEWTONIAN MECHANICS IS A
COMPLETED THEORY. . . .
THERE IS A WIDE REALM OF EXPERIENCES, OF OBSERVABLE
PHENOMENA,
THAT CAN BE DESCRIBED WITH HIGH ACCURACY BY MEANS OF
THIS SYSTEM. . . .
BUT THERE ARE OTHER REALMS OF EXPERIENCE."

—WERNER HEISENBERG

S: I developed the foundations of economics using what was believed about the nature of humankind at the time; the understanding now available did not exist then!

Q: Yes, you put forth your ideas on economics at a time when the only science was physics—which had recently separated from (natural) philosophy. There was no theory of living systems, no statistical theory, and no psychology, and in particular, no science of (human) consciousness.

S: Yes, everyone was quite taken with what Newton had done.

Q: Then it is understandable how and why economics came to have a mechanistic and materialistic foundation—it was a reflection of the times.

S: So, given the knowledge from these other new sciences, how should economics be?

Q: It should be evolutionary.

S: Why do you say that?

Q: Well, as we've established, the economic system not only serves the material needs of society, but, being a social system, it also affects human development—and not just in a material sense. Therefore, the precepts of economic practice should not only be consistent with the essence of humankind, it should facilitate human development.

S: You say that the economic system affects human development. What does this imply in regard to the system itself?

Q: If a system has influence on human evolution, then it must not be limiting to the individual.

S: How would such a system be so that it is not limiting, so that it facilitates human development?

Q: A social system such as an economy provides the context of life in society, it circumscribes experience. Hence, to be evolutionary, the system must not cause individuals to focus solely on one dimension or one aspect of life and not cause individuals to attach to things.

S: How can this be ensured?

Q: Well, the one thing we should keep in mind is that if we make anything necessary—making something a "must be"—then that which "must be" should be an internal dynamic and not an external static.

S: Why this distinction?

Q: When we develop attachments to things—like material wealth—then our focus will necessarily ignore all other dimensions in life, specifically the nonmaterial. Moreover, as we've previously discussed, because material gain is not without limits, its accomplishment can't be realized by everyone.

S: But isn't it societal wealth that affords people in society the means to meet their needs?

Q: Yes, but the needs you speak of are material or physiological needs. If we place our attention solely on the material aspects of life, then we necessarily ignore and thus forsake our own development as human beings.

S: Why do you say that?

Q: This is exactly what is happening in the current system; people are striving to gain all they can for themselves—becoming quite greedy—and the greater good is not being served.

S: The greater good is being served: The society has realized tremendous wealth! What greater good would be served if not the growth in wealth of the nation?

Q: The development of people; the evolution of humankind! What could be more important than this?

S: Are you saying that economics should not involve or concern itself with material wealth?

Q: No, I'm not saying that material production and societal wealth should not be a concern of economics; I am saying that it shouldn't be the sole concern.

S: Economic activity produces goods and services, which are material: What else is there other than material productivity?

Q: Nonmaterial productivity, human development! Creating and making goods and services involves both material and nonmaterial productivity, but the focus of our current economic system rests solely on that which is material.

Economic production involves the interplay of subjects and objects, of people and things. Thus economic activity does not only require labor it requires human engagement, and as a result it circumscribes human life.

S: I don't quite understand.

Q: Because it directly affects our understanding of life in practice—how to live and what to strive for and achieve in life—it plays a significant role in what we believe we are and what we believe we can become—the realization of human potential. Thus the sole focus on the pursuit of material wealth is limiting and too narrow to adequately serve humanity, to provide the facilitating context for human development.

S: Aren't you asking too much of economics? Why shouldn't it simply and solely speak to the production of goods and services?

Q: We can't slice up life into neat independent compartments; we can't disconnect what is inextricably connected. The production of goods and services clearly meets our physiological needs but it also affords each person the opportunity to express his/her unique talents and capabilities in and through his/her work.

S: Why can't people express their talents through hobbies or recreational activity?

Q: They surely can! And why does work have to be humanly unproductive? Must work be a brutish endeavor?

Is it an inherent requirement of the production of goods and services that work must not serve or cannot serve the interior and developmental needs of people?

S: No, it is not inherent, but generally people work just for the money.

Q: Yes they do, and that's my point: The system's design influences this but it need not be this way! The system was our creation—not a divine creation—and we can recreate it to better align with our very nature.

Each person has a developmental path to travel; each has unique capabilities to develop and share; engaging in economic activity can facilitate this unfolding. In this way, contributing to the production of goods and services would be a means to the development of the individual and in turn the betterment of society.

S: So where does the pursuit of one's material self-interest come into play?

Q: It seems as though you are trying to understand what I am saying while at the same time holding on to the thought that we are each created to maximize personal material gain. You are trying to understand a new idea by viewing it through the lens of an old idea, which doesn't allow you to see the idea without bias. You must let go of this thought if you want to (fully) understand the basis and merit of an alternative system of economics.

S: Doesn't the pursuit of self-interest afford opportunity for creativity and inventiveness?

Q: To a limited degree I can understand how you might conclude this; however, our creative capacity does not come from things out there, rather it emerges from within us, from within our very being.

S: But isn't our creativity sparked by things out there—by material circumstances and situations?

Q: Yes, the material world can and does provide the context within which creative inspiration emerges. However, creativity, a rupturing of *what is*, would be inhibited if there is an attachment to *what is*. That is, material self-interested behavior causes people to focus attention and develop an attachment to *what is*. Actually *what is* is usually the last impediment to realizing *what can be*.

S: But look at the wonderful technological advancements we've had; how can you say that material self-interested behavior wasn't the cause?

Q: Let's remember that technology is the application of knowledge and knowledge is increased through the sharing of ideas in dialogue—a collaboration—among different perspectives and not through independent self-interested behavior.

S: But isn't the desire to create the result of an individual pursuing his/her material self-interest?

Q: Your question seems to assume or imply that creativity is caused by self-serving forces. To the contrary, creativity emerges when the mind is open to exploring the possibilities; a mind not restricted by ego-consciousness or social context.

S: So the ego can't be creative?

Q: Creativity requires a playfulness of mind, which, as Aldous Huxley (1945, p. 35) asserted, is achieved "only by the annihilation of the self-regarding ego."

Consider that the creative process involves unconstrained exploration in thought; it involves a playfulness with ideas involving thinking that is not mediated by categories of thought or constrained by existing concepts or theories. In other words, creativity emerges when the mind is open to exploring the possibilities and not restricted by ego-consciousness or social context.

S: The egoic mind is not a creative mind?

Q: Yes, because the ego self-identifies by attaching to materialized (aspects of) reality, it finds it extremely difficult to suspend what it knows. The ego cannot put aside what it defines itself by—to forget itself—to enable the mind to take in and play with ideas that challenge the way things are—what it identifies with. So when it comes to anything involving attachments, the egoic mind will not be able to see anew. Just imagine how creative our society could be if this were not so! This is why it is so important for the economic system to be evolutionary.

S: You mentioned this before and I am still a bit unclear what you mean by the economic system being evolutionary.

Q: My use of the term is intended to communicate that the system would foster creative advancement. That said, I understand that the term "evolutionary" may not fully communicate what underlies this and so perhaps another descriptor would be "ecological." That is, since the system of economics must concern itself with the relationship among organizations and the environments (they so depend on) to ensure a continuous and healthy flow of energy for creativity to emerge, the addition of the term "ecological" might more clearly communicate this. More specifically, for us to preserve life and to evolve as a species, the meeting of both our physical (biological) and psychological needs require the perpetual flow of energy; an economic system that can facilitate this will best serve our interests.

S: I can understand the physical energy or material resource requirements for economic activity but I don't quite understand where or how energy fits with psychological needs.

Q: Let us take a step back to think further and more deeply about what we are discussing. You say you understand the need for material resources and physical energy in economic activity. Why is this so readily understood?

S: Material resources and physical energy go hand in hand.

Q: What do you mean "go hand in hand"?

S: The manufacture and production of goods requires raw material and energy to turn them into products for consumption.

Q: And when we speak of employing nature as a means to serving our economic needs, it is important to understand that nature is not simply immutable or inert matter in motion but rather it is alive and everything in it is a manifestation of exchanging and transforming energy.

In fact, energy is not attached to material resources, material resources are energy—matter-energy. If energy wasn't inherent in matter, then matter couldn't produce it—basically from nothing can come nothing.

S: Are you saying that matter and energy are not two things but rather one?

Q: Our entire universe and all that it contains is a manifestation of a self-regulating dynamic flow of energy—it might help to think of it as an energic system. We see reality comprised of forms, but we aren't consciously aware that what we perceive as reality is simply the flow of energy taking different forms.

S: Since, as you stated, energy flows, transforms, and manifests in different forms, this seems to be one way of explaining why reality changes.

Q: Yes, and it also helps us understand how our use of energy affects its availability and usefulness in the future.

S: Do you mean if we use too much we can use it up? I assumed our natural resources were limitless!

Q: Nature's processes are cyclical not limitless: We can use them up if the rate of use exceeds nature's rate of renewal and/or if the form to which it is transformed is for all intents and purposes unusable. Moreover, we now know from the first law of thermodynamics that we can't create or destroy energy, we can only transform it; in using it we alter its form and impact its future availability.

S: If energy can't be destroyed, then why wouldn't it always be available for our purposes?

Q: The amount may remain the same but its form will have changed by our use of it; and not all forms of energy are directly available and/or reusable. Although nature's processes recycle energy, as previously noted its renewal rate is not always commensurate with our rate of consumption.

S: So the energy in nature's resources (matter-energy) is not limitless.

Q: Yes, and moreover, when some forms of used energy are returned to and become concentrated in the environment they can inhibit the flow of energy—they can pollute the environment—which negatively affects our ability to not only sustain economic activity, but more important to sustain life healthfully. In fact the amount of energy rendered unusable for future use is known as entropy; the greater the entropy the less viable life becomes.

S: So the relationship between the economy and the environment should not be one of dominance, but rather it should be one of harmony—interdependence.

Q: Nature does not exist for humankind to exploit; and the same is true in regard to psychic-energy.

S: I don't understand the parallel you are making. When we employ the labor of another we aren't affecting the environment.

Q: There are two environments, the exterior and the interior. Although abuse and misuse of humankind can influence our external environment—sociocultural decay after all does have its causes—let's restrict our focus to the interior environment.

With regard to our interior, as we previously discussed, human beings are not complete at birth and therefore considerable development is required for them to mature. This development of self is greatly dependent on the productivity of the experiences afforded the individual in living his/her life. Clearly, participation in society's economy provides a large proportion of these experiences.

S: Economic activity is focused on the production of goods and services; it doesn't concern itself with human development!

Q: Well, that's exactly my point!

S: So we are back to the notion that contributing to the production of goods and services can be a means to the development of the individual and in turn to the betterment of society?

Q: Yes, it is all deeply interconnected. When energy gets dammed up— whether it physical/matter-energy or psychic/human-energy—it can't help but become toxic (we call it pollution) and unwholesome; it can't help but affect life adversely.

S: Can you explain how the economic system affects the flow of psychic/ human-energy?

Q: As we've established, the current economic system essentially rests on egocentrism, providing the context for material self-interested behavior. However, as previously discussed, material self-interested behavior causes people to focus attention on, and to develop an attachment to the pleasures found in material reality and such attachments block or inhibit the flow of psychic/human-energy, which adversely affects the development of ones' sense of self.

S: Yes, I recall our previous discussion but I do not quite understand its relationship to psychic/human-energy.

Q: If we use Maslow's (1945) hierarchy of needs as a framework to illustrate this point, we can see how when an individual becomes attached to some aspect of material reality he/she essentially becomes stuck at the lower level needs (i.e., physiological, security, belongingness, esteem, self-actualization) and ceases progressing toward self-actualization, the highest level in the hierarchy.

S: I am not familiar with Maslow's hierarchy, could you explain?

Q: Basically, Maslow advanced the notion that people's behavior could not be explained by stimulus– response mechanisms (by external forces) and that people inherently strive to realize their fullest potential—to make actual their potential. In the process of reaching the highest level need, each person must satisfy his/her lower level needs, which begin with the basic biological/physiological needs for food, water, oxygen, and so on. People seek to meet the next level of needs in the hierarchy as the previous level's needs are satisfied.

S: I think I understand, the levels correspond to different levels of concern?

Q: Yes, they do correspond with deeper levels of concern and correlative with increasing levels of self-awareness and higher levels of human capability.

S: Is someone who is realizing the highest level need—self-actualization—more human than one who is at the second or third level?

Q: Irrespective of whether he/she is meeting the lower level or the highest level needs, the individual is human; it is just that those who function at the highest level are realizing more of his/her unique humanness. For example, a person would realize greater human capability, say more creativity, if the higher level is attained.

S: So how does this align with our discussion on psychic/human-energy?

Q: When we focus our attention on something we are essentially directing our consciousness, making it a stronger part of our life. Hence mindful attention directs the flow of energy, canalizing psychic energy, and greatly influencing the way we behave in the world.

S: You have me a little confused: Can you be more specific?

Q: Consider one of the aspects of the safety/security level of needs is the need to have financial means. If an individual is materially focused, then he/she would seek need satisfaction by placing his/her attention on the material aspects of life.

S: This makes sense because financial wealth is a material need!

Q: Yes, and it does afford security and the means to attend to other basic needs. Now with the security need met, the materialistic person would seek to meet his/her esteem needs—the need for recognition and reputation—materially as well.

S: I don't understand what difference it makes as long as the need is satisfied and the individual can turn to realizing the next-level need.

Q: So, you are saying it would be okay for a person to be materially oriented in meeting each level of need in the hierarchy.

S: Why not! As long as a person's needs are met, he/she could progress to the next level of need toward self-actualization.

Q: But when materially oriented—with no natural satiation point—an individual can never quite obtain satisfaction; with no natural satiation point, a person would never feel that he/she has enough. Recall that the levels of need correspond with higher levels of concern, increasing levels of self-awareness, and the higher levels of human capability. With a material-based concern, attention remains at the lower level—in a sense energy flow is blocked.

S: This blocking of energy flow, would it be a form of pollution?

Q: Yes, precisely. Blocked up energy diminishes the likelihood of development—it is detrimental to self-actualization, to the development of the human spirit.

S: So how the need is met is as important as that the need is met?

Q: Yes, especially when taking a long view. With the pursuit of greater awareness being replaced with the pursuit of greater wealth, human development is suboptimized. There is a difference between merely meeting needs and seeking self-actualization. Also one is never secure since a material-oriented sense of security is fleeting because it is dependent on the size of one's material possessions, which can be lost or taken away and often determined by the decisions of others.

S: So the materially oriented are not likely to realize self-actualization!

Q: What we are saying is such individuals would be inhibited from becoming so because of their attachment to gaining increasing amounts of material wealth just to feel secure and/or to uphold their position and outward image. In so doing the development of one's bank account, for example, supplants the development of one's self; life becomes all about having and not about being.

S: I think I understand. We are talking about life while economics is concerned with the material needs of society.

Q: What is more critical to society than to have its members—your son, your daughter, your self—experiencing the joy of actualizing their uniquely human potential? What could be better for serving the greater good! Moreover material self-interest—material gain—cannot be realized by everyone because it is finite and limited. The system is designed to fail most people, especially during times of material scarcity.

S: Are you suggesting that serving the development of people rather than material self-interest will better serve society?

Q: The pursuit of material self-interest as a precept rests largely on the assumption that human nature is at base egoistic, materialistic, and hedonistic. I don't think it makes much sense to relegate people to simply being intelligent animals. Moreover, that people haven't an innate desire for productivity and improvement or to imagine beyond "what is," apart from what external stimuli would dictate.

Holding this belief is tantamount to advancing the belief that all human action is, essentially, reaction. That is, that people haven't an innate desire for productivity and improvement or to imagine beyond "what is," apart from what external stimuli would dictate. This belief system is incongruent with and is the antithesis of human development—it disregards humans as consciously aware beings with all the corresponding emergent powers, as we've previously discussed.

S: This may be true but doesn't the pursuit of self-interest serve the productivity of people and the industriousness of society?

Q: Actually new business ideas are generally about serving the needs of others, not serving one's self. Specifically, in the beginning when there are little material resources at hand it is the passion and commitment to an idea that enables entrepreneurial success, not self-interested behavior.

The new economic system we are exploring is grounded in the notion that each individual has within him/her a unique potential that through life's activities—in particular, economic activities—can be realized. But if the focus of the system is on time-bound materiality, such as wealth accumulation, then the system will limit the potential inherent in the human spirit. For economics to be ecological and correspondingly evolutionary it must support the long view; it must not lead us to confuse means with ends.

S: Where does activity in pursuit of greater wealth and profit fit in?

Q: These are means, not ends. If the system is intended for the amassing of material wealth and profit, then each individual would (unavoidably) become a means to another's end, making it necessary to invoke some level of mastery over others, as well as over nature. This would inhibit the expression of one's unique potential.

S: I understand you to be saying that if a necessary condition required an attachment to something unpredictable, like material reality, or if it fostered short-term thinking, then it would make the economic system nonevolutionary.

Q: That's right. Although we would have free enterprise and people would be free to pursue wealth accumulation—free to pursue the material self-interest, just like everyone else—they wouldn't be free to be and become what they potentially are as people's freedom would be limited to pursuing only the material aspects of life.

S: In a free-enterprise system each individual has a choice, do they not!

Q: While the choice of the enterprise may be free, the choices of the individual are not so much. The precept of egoistic economics is that people seek to maximize material self-interest, and with human nature not being inherently materialistic, everyone is required to desire the same thing, material wealth. Where is the individuality in that?

S: But each seeking his/her own gain in total would result in greater societal wealth.

Q: This is not the whole story; you are overlooking the unintended consequences.

S: What other results are there?

Q: What we have now: A highly skewed distribution of wealth, with its corresponding levels of poverty and working poor. People striving to have more rather than seeking to be more and government striving to regulate unfettered material self-interest. With a narrow focus on unlimited material growth, we exclude everything else. More specifically, with the focus isolated on "my gain," everyone is viewed instrumentally as a means to "my" material self-interest. People are viewed and treated as means, not ends. Instead, what I'm suggesting is a system with a unifying intent, not a polarizing intent. I am advancing the development or unfolding of humankind as the overarching intent and not, selfishly, anyone's or any group's material gain.

S: But aren't you arguing for socialism over capitalism, collectivism over individualism?

Q: No. Not in the sense of what Karl Marx advocated. What he advanced was a subordination of an individual's labor to the subsistence needs of society—to a central authority, the state. If you think further about this, in effect it isn't all that different from what our Western capitalistic system requires—people must consume to feed the system, a subordination of the individual.

I'm suggesting that each and every individual, being a unique expression of the human spirit, must be enabled to pursue the unfolding of his/her unique talents and capabilities.

S: It sounds very much like you are saying that individuals would be serving humankind, so why isn't that subordination?

Q: Because we each are human, serving humankind is serving ourselves—it is serving our greater self. This flows out of the fact that being human means being both an individual and a social being at the same time—what I am suggesting speaks to our "whole-partness." Each individual has a responsibility to develop his/her unique capabilities and to develop humanly productive relationships with other individuals as well.

S: Whole-part? I am not familiar with this term, what does it mean?

Q: We each are individual whole persons—whole entities—as well as parts of a larger whole, of a greater entity namely, humankind. In short we are whole-parts.

S: So we are individuals and members of the society within which we live—this is not different from what was assumed in my theory of political economy.

Q: Underlying your assertion is the assumption that humankind and society are synonymous: they are not.

Let me try to explain. People are constituent parts of humankind as well as members of a society/nation, but being a constituent part and being a member is not the same thing. We can't choose to be a constituent part of something else, but we can choose to be a member of a society/nation.

S: So no matter which society we are members of we are always simultaneously individual people and collectively constituents of humankind.

Q: Yes, we simultaneously are an "I" and a "We."

S: So why wouldn't serving our self-interest be the same as serving humankind? Or serving society the same as humankind?

Q: I suspect your notion of self-interest is based on the belief that each person is an independent being unto him/herself—the self as the lesser egoic self that we've previously spoken about. As an individual human being and as a constituent part of humankind we have a simultaneous responsibility to each; the responsibility to develop the self and the responsibility to contribute to the development of others.

S: Why then can't a person just focus on his/her self and let the invisible hand take care of the other?

Q: I think experience has shown that the invisible hand is a bit too invisible, nonexistent. More to the point, doing so would subordinate or ignore one for the other and the development of both is essential to human progress.

In spite of our individual differences, we are not separate, and so an economic system in service to humanity means that it must not divide or separate what is whole—it must not be divisive by promoting an egoic concern for self. Also, it mustn't facilitate the subordination of the individual to society; which is particularly devastating when society's beliefs and values-in-practice are not fully congruent with the goal of enabling the full expression of the human spirit.

Serving humankind rests on the notion that each person is a unique expression of the one spiritual essence and by each realizing and sharing the gift of his/her unique talents he/she in effect advances the development of humankind.

That is, with this system, material production would be an instrument—the means—to the evolvement of humankind, and not the other way around, as it is in our current egoistic economics.

S: I see this is about not confusing means with ends. But in the conduct of affairs, shouldn't economics be more concerned with justice and not benevolence?

Q: I assume you are saying that we should first take care of ourselves in economic affairs while not doing injustice to others; that what in the moment concerns the self should be our overriding concern.

S: Yes, that's what I am suggesting.

Q: In human affairs, I am not advocating benevolence over justice—it is not an either/or issue, it requires both. Given our interconnectedness, unavoidably, helping another helps our (greater) self and by doing an injustice to another, we do the self an injustice. But what we must be careful of is overextending our benevolence. We each need help from others in our unfolding, but in overextending our help we create dependency, which is actually detrimental to our unfolding.

S: If economics serves material growth and human development, how would you know that this economic system is producing growth? How would you know it is working?

Q: Instead of using the concept of growth as the criterion (such as increase in GDP or any number of metrics for the amount of accumulated material growth) as the primary measure of the system's performance, I suggest we turn our attention to the idea of progress.

S: Progress? How is this different than wealth accumulation and material growth?

Q: Progress, in the sense that I'm using it, is concerned with the present relative to the future. It is about a probable future, where the future is a higher state of human existence. It is about forward movement and enabling the birth of something new and beneficial.

     Growth, on the other hand, is about the present relative to the past. It is a material related or physical concept with dimensions that address size, quantity, weight, and power. Further, growth is bounded by the materiality of nature, whereas progress, which involves the manifestation of human potential, is only limited by one's finitude, which is transcended when we consider future generations.

S: Sorry, but I don't see the distinction you are making. Wouldn't it be progress if we accumulated a vast amount of wealth, making us a greater economic power? Haven't we made progress with the current economic system?

Q: There is no doubt that we (the United States) have become an economic force in the world through the tremendous wealth we've been able to amass. But, as some would argue, we did so without concern for the future. We've garnered great wealth by instrumentally using people and nature; we haven't progressed in a human way, only materially.

     If I can use a body-builder as metaphor, we've developed economic muscle by mistreating our parts (people) with our use of steroids (material self-interest). We have destroyed our health for the amassing of wealth. How irrational!

S: But doesn't progress include material as well as nonmaterial aspects?

Q: Yes: It encompasses both material and spiritual profit.

S: So how is progress realized, if not by the pursuit of unlimited material growth?

Q: By enabling each person to realize or express his/her potential, as well as to take responsibility for his/her way of being-in-the-world. As previously discussed, in so doing each individual contributes to the progress (evolution) of humankind.

S: The empiricist in me wants to know how you measure progress, if not by the amount of productivity and wealth realized; if not by the monetary gain afforded over a particular period of time.

Q: Although a complete answer to your question would take us beyond the scope of this discussion, we can provide a glimpse of what it might entail. But first a caution: In practice, in addressing this we must be very careful not to misplace the symbol for the concrete reality. That is, we must not let our measures take us away from the concrete individuals or human activities involved. After all, it is the progress of humankind that the system is to serve, not the growth or movement in some abstract measure or indicator.

S: Can you expand on this a little?

Q: Consider for the moment that we wish to measure the efficacy of the system (i.e., the greater good realized). Let's say we use wealth as a quantifiable measure by attaching a numerical (monetary) value to what has been produced, for which the numeric we assign reflects the amount of resources and hours of human effort expended in production of a commodity. Because the abstract representation (i.e., monetary unit) we use to represent the societal good can be compounded endlessly, we can mistakenly think that the amount of resources and human effort can be compounded correspondingly without limit—the illusion of unlimited growth is thereby reinforced in the process.

The mistake we would be making is to think that the measure, the quantity with which we represent the greater societal good, is the concrete reality. Our measure doesn't reflect the fullness of what we seek, yet we treat it as if it does. In so doing, we ignore, forget, and make abstract the very human reality from which it came and which it is to serve. This error becomes magnified in exchange (i.e., transactions) when we inflate the value of what was produced for self-serving reasons.

(One has to wonder if it is likely that this could contribute to the phenomenon of inflation, simply because accumulated wealth can often be realized without commensurate human effort.)

S: It seems that this could happen with anything that is quantified. How can you avoid it?

Q: Well, completely avoiding it may be impossible, but minimizing it is well within the realm of possibility. We can do this by never losing sight of the fact that the system is to serve concrete people and that our measures, at best, are only partial and incomplete representations. The numbers are never the reality!

S: I see. Can we get back to my initial question about empirical evidence of the system's efficacy?

Q: Staying with the dimension of greater societal good in the production of a commodity, what needs to be done is to include the material as well as the nonmaterial benefits and burdens associated with a commodity's production. We would include both public and private consequences as well as the intended and unintended consequences. That is, not only do we include the monetary value derived in exchange, but also the dis-economies generated—both current and future.

S: Are you suggesting that we not measure the value realized in the production of goods?

Q: No. I am advocating that we not focus solely on the resultant material value generated from production. Borrowing an idea from Thorstein Veblen, we ought to include the value derived through the process of production; that is to say, what is generated in the process of production that is of human value? For example, our measures should include surrogates or correlates of trust, honesty, respect, cooperation, harmony, love, self-responsibility/self-directedness.

S: Why do we need to be concerned about these subjective issues? Economics is about commerce, it is about producing goods and services, is it not?

Q: It's important to distinguish between productivity in Western capitalism (egoistic economics) and productivity in ecological/evolutionary economics. In the former, the focus is materially centered and in the latter it is human-centered and far more integrated with the whole of life.

Reflected in the measures used in egoistic economics is evidence that we don't much care about what is produced or how it is produced, as long as it contributes to greater material wealth. The ends of greater wealth, justifies any means.

Our economic indicators include the production of detrimental goods and services to humankind as positive contributors to economic growth. Egoistic economic theory makes no distinction in regards to what is exchanged—whether we produce necessities or narcotics, gum or guns, it is all the same—in the accounting all that counts is the wealth created through the transactions. For example, the production of tobacco products, along with the health costs associated with treating people with related medical problems adds positively to the GDP. Seems to be somewhat misleading, doesn't it?

S: Well, a bit. But that's why we have laws to control and oversee unjust activity.

Q: There is so much that goes on that is not against the law but yet that obstructs the evolvement of the individual. We must include the effects of these practices in our measures to make them the focus of our attention. The important point is that in economic activity, we must be able to capture the effects of actions that are counter to human progress.

S: You're suggesting that a business whose management was detrimental to the development of its employees would contribute negatively to progress even though it may add considerably to the GDP and generate a sizable amount of profit?

Q: Yes, exactly that! The production of humanly detrimental products and services or the use of processes of production and methods of management that are detrimental to the evolution of humankind must be captured as negative contributions to progress. In this way an industry or business enterprise would be identified by its contribution to human progress—the material monetary contribution should no longer be the sole yardstick.

For example, Clifford Cobb, Ted Halstead, and Jonathan Rowe (1995) suggest the use of an indicator they call the Genuine Progress Indicator (GPI) to monitor economic well-being. The GPI is a much broader index than the GDP, as it captures transactions that add to well-being as well as those that diminish well-being. Needless to say, it hasn't replaced the GDP.

Is measuring progress simple and straightforward? No! Is it important? I believe it is, for our measures influence the focus of our attention and subsequently, our way-of-being-in-the-world.

In economic affairs, we must be able to capture the effects of the use of intelligence in the absence of wisdom. Without the appropriate focus of attention our actions become destructive, especially with the application of more advanced technology.

S: What you describe is a radical change from what is currently done.

Q: Yes. But what is currently done is grounded in a very narrow and limiting view of humankind, which doesn't contribute to our humanness and its development.

There is no divine law that tells us that the current system is necessary; it can be otherwise! In fact the only thing that supports its continuance is the theory itself–rather nonevolutionary, wouldn't you say? If we wish to become what we potentially are, then radical change is needed. Let us not forget, progress presupposes change—you can't have progress without it!

S: With this shift in economic theory, how will the role of labor change?

Q: Let's first establish that people (labor) and the economic system are in mutual relation.

S: Mutual relation?

Q: Mutual relation means that they affect each other—there is significant interdependence.

S: The influence being that the productivity of labor contributes to the effectiveness of the economy and the wealth of a nation.

Q: Yes, but the influence proceeds in both directions—it is not simply unidirectional and linear. In society, the institution of economics greatly influences people's thinking and norms of behavior. What I'm saying is that in defining the relationship, we must recognize the influence that the economic system has on people's way of being-in-the-world, which in turn influences progress.

S: I've noted that in every improved society labor's productivity was the major contributor. This led to me advocating division of labor as the means to enhance labor's productivity and, in turn, the material wealth of the nation.

How does this fit with ecological/evolutionary economic thought?

Q: In traditional economic thought, societal improvement is synonymous with gains in the material productivity of its labor and resources. Accordingly, the sole purpose of people's work is to serve the productivity goals of the business enterprise. Essentially, people are working for the economic system.

S: Employing labor, according to the requirements of the economic system, is a way for people to acquire the means to get what they desire. After all, people are paid a wage for their labor.

Q: So, what people derive from their work is the satisfaction of their material needs. But, as we've discussed, people are more than intelligent animals with material needs who are capable of laboring as directed. People also have the inherent need to become more of what they potentially are; and the likelihood of this happening significantly increases in an ecological/evolutionary economic system. People ought to get more from their work than monetary gain.

S: Just how is the relationship with labor different in ecological/evolutionary economics?

Q: In ecological/evolutionary economics, just as in the current egoic system, people play a critical role in the production of goods and services. However, there are two dimensions to productivity, material productivity and human productivity, the latter refers to the growth and development of the individual. If all that people get out of their work is a paycheck—things of outer value—then the fullness of their humanity is not being served—in short, people aren't being humanly productive.

Failing to attain a mutually beneficial relationship between the system and the people will be detrimental to humankind. Clearly engagement in economic activity should prove profitable, humanly (spiritually) as well as materially.

S: I don't quite understand. People are hired to perform a specific task or job and in return the employer (a business enterprise) pays for their labor. This is economics; what else is there?

Q: Work is not just a means for gaining income—at least it should not be given the human condition. People cannot simply exist and be human. Not using our capabilities, not interacting and engaging with other humans tends to alienate a person and diminishes development. In short, our humanness must be realized in the acts of life, and a central activity in life is work. Engaging in meaningful work provides an opportunity to exercise and stretch the mind and to derive the benefit of inner value from work.

S: I understand work providing economic value, but what would be something of inner value?

Q: Joy.

S: So work that is joyful is more satisfying?

Q: Joy is not a by-product of job satisfaction; nor are joy and satisfaction synonymous. Joy is inherent in the activity of the work itself; it is derived from what the work is, not from what the work gives relative to expectation.

S: Can you explain what might constitute inherently joyful work?

Q: Work that enables people to learn and engage their creativity.

S: Why do these engender joy?

Q: Engaging in learning and in the creative process provide us the opportunity to tap into and use our uniquely human capabilities. What this means is that engaging in the processes of learning and creativity we experience (a greater sense of) our humanness—a sense of human fulfillment—thus joy is felt.

S: What's the effect when we experience joy in work?

Q: At least two benefits are derived: (1) when we engage fully in the activity of our work we tend to produce quality and (2) we can only develop our humanity—become more of what we are—when we are in touch with our humanness. In short we must first realize our humanness before we can become more human.

S: So you are saying that in the process of work the opportunity for learning and creativity must be provided for people to fully develop as human beings.

Q: Yes, and this has implications for the division of labor. If labor is divided in such a way as to result in alienation, reduced meaning, and increased fragmentation of work, then creativity is less likely to emerge. Moreover, if the management of the business doesn't honor the individual and promote and build trust, then fear will emerge; and the presence of fear inhibits creativity. Also, if there is an overemphasis placed on quantity of production (i.e., material productivity), to the exclusion of quality, then this too will diminish the emergence of creativity. With the absence of learning and creative opportunities, we inhibit human development and as a result, the productivity realized ceases to be humanly productive. In our material gain, we all lose.

S: From your description, it sounds as though in this system people are to concern themselves with the needs of others as well.

Q: Because the economic system influences the thoughts and behavior of people, in ecological/evolutionary economic thought, self-interest is not limited to the egoic self, but rather more fully to the greater self—a self inextricably connected to all selves. Selfish behavior becomes selfless behavior.

S: If benevolent, what place is there for the free-market enterprise?

Q: For services and commodities produced, the market system can afford everyone the opportunity to share in the fruits of each others' talents. But for developing people's talents, I don't believe the market system affords the best mechanism.

S: If it works for commodities, then why not for labor?

Q: Let's not forget that labor is in reality people. If, in a similar manner, we apply the market system to people, then we make them a commodity—viewing others as means to our ends—which would be counterproductive to human evolvement.

S: But every person lives by exchanging.

Q: In the exchange within the egoistic system, the employer seeks to give as little wage as possible, whereas the employee seeks to realize as much wage as possible—in the labor market each is seeking to maximize his/her egoic self-interest.

S: Of course, how else can we attain the natural price of our talents, if not through the market?

Q: Natural price? The idea that there exists a natural price, especially for one's talents, is questionable; it presupposes a determinism, that price exists independent of context and prior to the experience. You see, this mechanism with its emphasis on price and material value disregards the human value each provides to everyone who is served by the individual's talents.

S: Human value? Don't you mean use value?

Q: In the exchange we must not focus solely on the objective aspects of the transaction, but appreciate that all human interaction is (inter)-subjective; more is exchanged than just commodities and money. In a transaction between people, aspects of intersubjective value are also exchanged, such as trust and respect. These may not contribute to wealth, but they do contribute to wholeness and our development as human beings—they contribute to progress.

S: I am a bit confused with this notion of intersubjectivity: What are you saying?

Q: Given the interconnectedness of the self with all other selves, self-interest takes on a completely different meaning and, therefore, employers seeking to drive down wages as low as possible, or employees seeking to maximize their material gain, would be self-destructive.

Furthermore, we must acknowledge that people seek to gain more from work than material gain. Human behavior cannot be explained by an algebraic equation, as human development cannot be fully quantified.

S: But *a person must always live by his/her work!*

Q: Yes, this is true. But it is also true that *people do not live by bread alone!*

An ecological/evolutionary system would recognize that every person survives by exchanging goods, but each truly lives by engaging in activities and interacting with others in a way that contributes to his/her development; people positively need activities and interactions that are vitalizing. So we might say that a person survives by his/her work, but only truly experiences (human) life through joyful work.

But, I believe we are getting beyond the purpose of our discussion of outlining the precepts of ecological/evolutionary economics. We will discuss this—evolutionary management—at another time.

Leadership for Progress

S: We've talked about quite a bit and my head is spinning: Can we briefly summarize what we've discussed and explore where this transformation can begin?

Q: Okay, let's try. The paradigmatic shift from egoistic economics to ecological/evolutionary economics involves a transformation of consciousness. It requires greater depth of understanding of what it means to be human and a corresponding shift in focus from the materiality of reality to the spirituality underlying reality.

S: This change is a change from believing that we are independent self-interested pain-avoiding and pleasure-seeking creatures, to realizing that we are each interconnected manifestations of the human spirit, seeking to become what we potentially are.

Q: Yes, and the economic system we create must facilitate this unfolding, recognizing that what we do to each other, we do to ourselves

S: Instead of primarily being concerned for the individual egoic self, we must seek to develop helping relationships. Benevolence is to replace egoic self-interest.

Q: To realize this, the intent of the system must change from unlimited material growth to human progress.

S: It seems as though you are saying that economic activity does not benefit us, especially in the long run.

Q: No, that's not at all what I am saying! But I understand how you could conclude this. Let's see if I can clarify.

With consideration of the relevance of economics to our well-being the critical question is, what (fundamental) human value or need are we seeking to realize through our engagement in economic activity, through out engagement in work?

S: Being pragmatic, the most important aspect is wealth. After all wealth makes it possible to serve our consumption needs, which are clearly dependent on society being economically productive. And doesn't this ecological/evolutionary perspective you are advocating place constraints on economic production?

Q: Of course we have to consume, and of course consumption requires production, but we must not misplace means for ends. The relationship begins with the need to consume, which in turn requires the need to produce—wealth is not an inherent human value/need.

Furthermore, when speaking to our need to consume we are referring to our subsistence/survival needs and the notion of unlimited pursuit of (material) self-interest does not logically follow, because our subsistence needs have an inherent satiation point—there is no inherent need for unfettered consumption.

I must ask, are we producing to maximize wealth or to meet an inherent human need?

S: What difference does it make? In doing one, we necessarily must do the other.

Q: Yes, consumption and production are interdependent, but as just previously mentioned it all begins with our subsistence/survival needs, which have their natural satiation points. Making it unnecessary to produce more than we need to consume.

S: In business don't we produce to meet demand? It seems that the ecological/evolutionary perspective you've described is a constraint to business. So, how does one get around the constraints that the ecological/evolutionary perspective places on production, on the conduct of business?

Q: Get around the constraints? You don't. Unfettered production for the sake of wealth accumulation is actually detrimental to humankind for it exacts far too great a toll.

The more we increase production, the more we need to increase consumption beyond what subsistence needs require. This in turn creates the greater need for want or egoic consumption. In an egoistic economic society, as our sense of self-worth is conditional on our ability to produce and consume, feelings of self-doubt and fear intensify, which causes us to seek relief by increasing our consumption, which in turn increases the demand for production.

However, the more we increase production, the more energy we consume and the greater the entropy (i.e., the less readily available energy there is for use by future generations). As energy becomes less available, and/or more difficult to access, the more costly are the goods and services we consume. Now, as costs increase, driving the price of goods upward, the greater the downward pressure on consumption and profit, which in turn, increases the desire to reduce the cost of goods and services—let us not forget in this paradigm the business of business is profit.

Ultimately this results in efforts to reduce costs further through efforts to pay less for labor, which unavoidably decreases consumer income and thus consumption—not surprisingly adversely affecting profit—which places downward pressure on production. An economic slowdown is never too far off in the future!

What's the bottom line? The engine of self-interest driving business and economic activity is destined to destroy the very system it created and depends on—it is a system that is nothing but suicidal! You see, the pursuit of unlimited growth and wealth accumulation is not a self-regulating process, but rather self-reinforcing toward self-destruction.

S: By this account egoic economics is itself ultimately a constraint on the economic viability of a society.

Q: Basically the issue is what should be the intent of business, to enable the development of humankind or enable the development of ego? What I am trying to say is that engaging in economic activity must be its own reward. If our intent is something other than the joint aims of self-preservation and self-transcendence, then humankind is merely instrumental to other ends, and the cycle turns increasingly harmful. With survival and evolvement as the intent, the ecological/evolutionary perspective affords guidance, not constraints.

The preservation of an environment affording sustainability and personal development should not be thought of as a constraint, for the society of humankind is not something else other than us! That's like saying that I find my need to continue to exist a to limit on me in the activities I engage in–I feel constrained by life's principles.

S: But can't the advances in technology change the dynamics you've outlined? Wouldn't the application of science either reverse the trend or, at least, negate any increase in entropy?

Q: I believe you're speaking of recycling, in which yesterday's products are used in tomorrow's production.

S: Yes, don't you have that capability today to do just this? Wouldn't we then have what is evident in nature, the capacity to reuse previously expended energy?

Q: First of all we have to align the rate of use with the energy-renewal rate. Second even the recycling process consumes energy, adding to entropy. It is not, and never can be, 100% restorative. Remember we can't create energy, we can only transform it.

S: I now see what is meant by relative autonomy. We must maintain harmony with our environment as we engage in economic activity so as to preserve our continued existence.

Q: Not only this, but we must manage our organizations in a way that is in harmony with our (human) nature.

S: Why is this so important? The work gets done and the products and services get produced just the same. Society gets what it needs and, so too, does the producer.

Q: But what about individuals and their development? Even though we may not be polluting the exterior environment, we may be polluting the interior environment by suppressing the expression of the human spirit.

S: How would we know whether we are polluting the interior environment?

Q: We have to look at whether people are relating as subjects or objects; whether relationships are based on love or fear; are relationships enabling or overpowering; do relationships contribute to the unleashing of the potential within the individual or are they restricting this expression?

S: Love! What does love have to do with the conduct of business?

Q: My use of the term "love"—borrowing from Erich Fromm—does not refer to anything sexual, but rather to everything human. By love, I mean the need we each have to be honored as an individual living being–as an expression of the one human spirit. It is because of this spiritual essence that we all have the need to be loved, for it is the pathway to our unfolding.

S: Are you speaking of benevolence—of which we spoke earlier?

Q: Yes. To love another, in the context within which I am speaking, is to have concern for the well-being of others, and to do this for no other reason but for the other's well-being—not for profit, not for self-image, not for anything other than authentic concern.

S: But doesn't this take a business enterprise away from its primary focus, the efficient conduct of its business?

Q: If an enterprise were to focus, as you say, principally on itself, then it would be committing a grave ecological error. Recall that the unit of survival is not the entity, but rather the entity plus its constituent whole-parts.

S: Suppose that an enterprise primarily concerned itself with its own interest, wouldn't it have a better chance of realizing greater success, given that all of its attention and efforts would be directed toward this end?

Q: What you are asking is, wouldn't the enterprise be better off if it limited its focus to itself? In this situation, the organization wouldn't be seeking to harmonize with its constituent holons (Koestler, 1967), but, in effect, it would be drawing a line between its interests and that of everyone else—an either me or them mind-set. It would create a competition between itself and its environments; a game that the enterprise would ultimately lose, especially when it wins.

The point I am trying to make is that it is not an either/or, me or them issue, but rather it is about recognizing that what appears as two separate entities is in reality one—different but not separate. That is, the enterprise doesn't exist without people; it doesn't survive if people can't survive; it can't adapt if people can't adapt; it can't be creative if people can't be creative; it can't flourish if people can't flourish. By limiting the focus to one's own interest, the focus, in effect, becomes limiting.

S: I think I understand. What would you suggest a business enterprise do?

Q: An enterprise must have the mind-set that its unit of survival is not the separate entity, but rather the enterprise plus its environments, which includes humankind. Accordingly, the focus of the enterprise would not be merely material or monetary in nature, rather, it would include the interior and exterior dimensions of reality.

S: What must happen for an enterprise to realize harmony with its environments?

Q: Those in authority must be human, and not merely executives of an economic machine. They must be responsible and acknowledge their role in human unfolding–theirs and ours. They must make a conscious choice to learn and to revere all that is alive; to never, ever, place material gain above human value. They must cease thinking of people and nature as resources to be instrumentally used for the achievement of goals of outer value. They must actually provide the leadership experience that we all need.

> [T]he most far reaching control possessed by any society
>   over its future
> is the power to remake its institutions.
>
> **—Sir Geoffrey Vickers**

> Evolution always follows the path of viability.
>
> **—Gregory Bateson**

Epilogue

The Madness of Our Pleasures

We've become powerless over our own creation; we serve it, rather than it serving us. We perpetuate the situation, not because we need to, but because we feel compelled to—our success, our socially mediated meaning in life is at stake. What choice do we have! The pressure of conformity to continue this way is enormous. If we have more, society will approve of us, but if we have less, or choose not to seek more, then disapproval will, most surely, follow. We will be thought of as irrational, weird— not normal! Yet we are told to think of ourselves as free individuals. The fact that we are hooked cannot be denied. We are living a reality that is driving us slightly mad.

We live in a society of contradictory objectives. Such a situation of contradiction is similar to what Gregory Bateson refers to as a double bind. For example, on the one hand we are told to seek our own material self-interests while at the same time we are told to live democratically (i.e., in a society of the people, by the people, and for the people) with concern for our fellow human beings. This double bind causes us to experience life in society as a contradiction. But it is a contradiction we are not allowed to discuss or even recognize, and one we cannot leave. The fact that we can't leave it is enough to make us slightly mad. All that we can do is escape (i.e., temporarily check-out) by losing or repressing our true selves by engaging in various forms of addictive consumption—numbing ourselves to the contradiction we live. Fully adapted to this socially patterned having mode of being in the world causes us to reject alternative ways of relating and living; we are unable to see beyond the immediacy of our hedonistic concerns—not beyond the pleasure-seeking and pain-avoidance mode of existence. We are unwilling to give up our illusory freedom.

As long as we maintain this habitual way of living—as long as we continue to follow the maxims of egoistic capitalism—we are headed in the direction of dissolution, not evolution: For we cannot possibly progress as a species when we are increasing our ego-strength and, correspondingly, relinquishing our uniquely human powers in service to the invisible authority of the economy. But, while leading ourselves to destruction, we will feel self-assured in the illusion of security and control, for conformity and familiarity of habit diminishes our awareness of uncertainty and doubt. The egoistic economy, by definition, is self-serving; it serves, but only itself. Cooperating with this system, in the end we all lose.

Because economic theory and practice touches much of life in society, what we've discussed has far-reaching implications. Government policy, finance, accounting, education, and business management, to name a few, will likely require major changes.

In future work we will explore these ideas in regard to how an enterprise would be organized and managed toward sustaining viability and facilitating the unfolding of our humanness. For our world to be a more human world, we must each commit to becoming more human.

Bibliography

Abell, P. (1996) A model of the informal structure (culture) of organizations. *Rationality & Society, 8* (4), 433–452.

Adler, P. S. (1996). Two types of bureaucracy: Enabling and coercive. *Administrative Science Quarterly. 41* (1), 61–89.

Bandrowski, J. (1990). *Corporate imagination plus.* New York: Free Press.

Barbour, I. (1997). *Religion and science: Historical and contemporary issues.* San Francisco, CA: HarperCollins.

Bateson, G. (1972). *Steps to an ecology of mind.* New York: Chandler Publishing Company.

Berger, P., & Luckmann, T. (1966). *The social construction of reality.* New York: Anchor Books.

Berman, M. (1984). *The re-enchantment of the world.* New York: Bantam Books.

Bohm, D. (1980). *Wholeness and the implicate order.* London: Routledge.

Bohm, D. (1994). *Thought as system.* New York: Routledge.

Bohm, D. (1998). *On creativity.* New York: Routledge.

Bohm, D., & Peat, D. (1987). *Science, order and creativity.* New York: Bantam.

Brown, N. O. (1959). *Life against death.* Middletown, CT Wesleyan University Press.

Checkland, P. (1993). *Systems thinking, systems practice.* New York: John Wiley & Sons.

Campbell, J. (1988). *The power of myth with Bill Moyers* (B. S. Flowers, Ed.). New York: Doubleday Dell.

Capra, F. (1977). *The tao of physics.* New York: Bantam Books.

Capra, F. (1996). *The web of life.* New York: Anchor Books.

Capra, F., & Steindl-Rast, D. (1991). *Belonging to the universe.* New York: HarperCollins.

Chopra, D. (1990). *Magical mind magical body* [audiotape]. Niles, IL: Nightingale-Conant Corporation.

Chopra, D. (1994). *The seven spiritual laws of success.* San Rafael, CA: Amber-Allen Publishing.

Chopra, D. (1997). *The path to love: Renewing the power of spirit in your life.* New York: Harmony Books.

Cobb, C., Halstead, T., & Rowe, J. (1995, October). If the GDP is Up, Why is America Down? *Atlantic Monthly.* Available athttp://www.theatlantic.com/politics/ecbig/gdp.htm

Csikszentmihalyi, M. (1993). *The evolving self.* New York: HarperCollins.

Csikszentmihalyi, M. (1996). *Creativity.* New York: HarperCollins.

Daly, H., & Cobb, J. B. (1994). *For the common good.* Boston, MA: Beacon Press

Davies, P. (1992). *The mind of God: The scientific basis for rational a world.* New York: Simon & Schuster.

Deikman, A. J. (1996). 'I' = Awareness. *Journal of Consciousness Studies, 3*(4), 350–356.Available: at http://www.imprint.co.uk/online/Deikman.html

Deming, W. E. (1986). *Out of the crisis.* Cambridge, MA: Massachusetts Institute of Technology Center for Advanced Engineering Study.

Deming, W. E. (1993). *The new economics.* Cambridge, MA: Massachusetts Institute of Technology Center for Advanced Engineering Study.

Descartes, R. (1960). *Discourse on method and meditations* (L. J. Lafleur, trans). New York: Bobbs-Merrill. (Original work published 1637)

Dossey, L. (1999). *Reinventing medicine.* San Francisco: HarperCollins.

Dreyfus, H. L. (1991). *Being-in-the-World* Cambridge, MA: MIT Press.

Eisler, R. (1987). *The chalice & the blade: Our history, our future.* New York: HarperCollins.

Eisler, R.,& Loye, D. (1990). *The partnership way.* New York: HarperCollins.

Etzioni, A. (1988). *The moral dimension.* New York: Free Press.

Feldman, S. P. (1997). The revolt against cultural authority: Power/knowledge as an assumption in organization theory. *Human Relations, 50* (8), 937–955.

Fox, M., & Sheldrake, R. (1997). *Natural grace.* New York: Image Books.

Friedman, M. (1962). *Capitalism and freedom.* Chicago: University of Chicago Press.

Fromm, E. (1941). *Escape from freedom.* New York: Holt, Rinehart & Winston.

Fromm, E. (1947). *Man for himself.* New York: Ballantine Books.

Fromm, E. (1955). *The sane society.* New York: Holt, Rhinehart & Winston.

Fromm, E. (1976). *To have or to be?* New York: Harper & Row.

Fukuyama, F. (1999). *The great disruption: Human nature and the reconstitution of social order.* New York: Free Press.

Galbraith, J. K. (1987). *Economics in perspective: A critical history.* Boston: Houghton Mifflin.

Gerogopoulos, N. & Heim, M. (Ed.). (1995). *Being human in the ultimate: Studies in the thought of John M. Anderson*. Atlanta, GA: Rodopi.

Goldberg, P. (1983). *The intuitive edge*. New York: Jeremy P. Tarcher/ Putnam Books.

Grosso, M. (1997). *Soulmaking*. Charlottesville, VA: Hampton Roads.

Hanline, M. (1993). *Human belief, rationality and social organization: A critique of organizational theory*. Gulph Breeze, FL: Matrix Publishers.

Hart, E. (1993). *The creative loop: How the brain makes the mind*. New York: Addison-Wesley.

Hausman, D. M. (1994). *The philosophy of economics: An anthology* (2nd ed). New York: Cambridge University Press.

Heil, J. (1998). *Philosophy of mind*. New York: Routledge.

Heilbroner, R. (1972). *The making of economic society* (4th ed.). Englewood Cliffs, NJ: Prentice-Hall.

Heilbroner, R. (1990). Analysis and vision in the history of modern economic thought. *Journal of Economic Literature*, *28*, 1097–1114.

Heisenberg, W. (1958). *Physics and philosophy*. New York: Harper Torch-books.

Hendry, J. (1999). Cultural theory and contemporary management organization. *Human Relations*, *52* (5), 557–577.

Hinings, C. R. (1996). Values and organizational structure. *Human* , *49* (7), 885–916.

Hock, D. (2000). The nature and creation of chaotic organizations. *Systems Thinker*, *11* (3), 1–4.

Hunt, E. K. (1992). *History of economic thought: A critical perspective* (2nd ed). New York: HarperCollins.

Huxley, A. (1945). *The perennial philosophy*. New York: Harper & Row.

Huxley, A. (1977). *The human situation*. New York: Harper & Row.

Ingram, D., & Simon-Ingram, J. (Eds.). (1992). *Critical theory*. New York: Paragon House.

Jacobi, J. (1973). *The psychology of C. G. Jung*. New Haven, CT: Yale University Press.

James, W. (1977). *The writings of William James* (J. J. McDermott,Ed.). Chicago: University of Chicago Press.

Jermier, J. M. (1998). Introduction: Critical perspectives on organizational control. *Administrative Science Quarterly*, *43*(2), 235–256.

Jung, C. G. (1960). *On the nature of the psyche* (R. F. C. Hull, trans.). Princeton, NJ: Princeton University Press.

Jung, C. G. (1964). *Man and his symbols*. New York: Dell Publishing.

Jung, C. G. (1971). *The portable Jung*. New York: Viking Press.

Kauffman, D. L., Jr. (1980). *An introduction to systems thinking* Minneapolis, MN: S. A. Carlton.

Kearins, K. (1996). Power in organizational analysis: Delineating and contrasting a Foucauldian perspective. *Electronic Journal of Radical Organizational Theory, 2* (2). Available at http://www.mngt.waikato.ac.nz/ejrot/

Kellner, D., & Best, S. (1991). *Postmodern theory*. New York: Guilford Press.

Koestler, A. (1967). *The ghost in the machine*.New York: Macmillan.

Kohn, A. (1990). *The brighter side of human nature*. New York: Basic Books.

Kohn, A. (1993). *Punished by rewards*. New York: Houghton Mifflin.

Korzybski, A. (1921). *Man and manhood*. Lakeville, CT: International Non-Aristotelian Library Publishing Company.

Krishnamurti, J. (1969). *Freedom from the known*. New York: HarperSanFrancisco.

Krishnamurti, J. (1978). *Truth and actuality*. New York: HarperSanFrancisco.

Laszlo, E. (1972). *The systems view of the world*. New York: George Braziller.

Leiss, W. (1994). *The domination of nature*. Montreal: McGill-Queen's University Press.

Leon, J. C. (1999). *Science and philosophy in the West*. Upper Saddle River, NJ:

Prentice-Hall.

Levine, L. (1998). Whole system design (WSD): The shifting focus of attention and the threshold challenge. *Journal of Applied Behavioral Science, 34* (3), 305–326.

Lewis, C. I. (1929). *Mind and the world order*. New York: Dover Publications.

Lao-tzu. (1988). *Tao te ching* (S. Mitchel, trans.). New York: Harper Collins.

Marsden, R., & Townley, B. (1995). Power and postmodernity: Reflections on the pleasure dome. *Electronic Journal of Radical Organizational Theory, 1* (1), Available at http://www.mngt.waikato.ac.nz/ejrot/

Maslow, A. H. (1943, July). A theory of human motivation. *Psychological Review*, 1943, pp. 370–396.

May, T. (1993). *Between genealogy and epistemology: Psychology, politics and knowledge in the thought of Michel Foucault*. University Park, PA: Pennsylvania State University Press.

McDermott, J. J. (1977). *The writings of William James*. Chicago: University of Chicago Press

McFadden, L M. (1998). Team concepts for emerging organizational architectures. *Information Outlook, 2* (12), 18–23.

McKinlay, A., & Starkey, K. (Eds). (1998). *Foucault, management and organization theory*. London: Sage .

Mill, J. S. (1892). *Principles of political economy*. New York: D. Appleton.

Miringoff, M., & Miringoff, Me-L. (1999). *The social health of the nation: How America is really doing.* New York: Oxford University Press.

Moore, T. (1992). *Care of the soul.* New York: HarperCollins.

Moore, T. (1996). *The re-enchantment of everyday life.* New York: HarperCollins.

Northhead, A. W. (1925). *Science and the modern world.* New York: Macmillan.

Polanyi, M. (1958). *Personal knowledge.* Chicago: University of Chicago Press.

Randall, J. H., Jr. (1940). *The making of the modern mind* (5th ed.). New York: Columbia University Press.

Russell, P. (1992). *The white hole in time: Our future evolution and the meaning of now.* San Francisco: HarperCollins.

Rhinelander, P. H. (1973). *Is man incomprehensible to man?* San Francisco: W.H. Freeman.

Rifkin, J. (1989). *Entropy: Into the green house world.* New York: Bantam Books.

Schaef, A. W., & Fassel, D. (1988). *The addictive organization.* New York: HarperCollins.

Schein, E. H. (1996). Culture: The missing concept in organization studies. *Administrative Science Quarterly, 41* (2). 229–240.

Schermerhorn, J. R., Jr. (1996). *Management* (5th ed.). New York: Wiley.

Schneider, H. K. (1974). *Economic man: The anthropology of economics.* New York: Free Press.

Screpanti, E., & Zamagni, S. (1993). *An outline of the history of economic thought.* New York: Oxford University Press.

Sheldrake, R. (1995). *A new science of life.* Rochester,VT: Park Street Press.

Sherburne, D. W. (1981). *A key to Whitehead's process and reality.* New York: Free Press.

Shewhart, W. (1939). *Statistical method: From the viewpoint of quality control.* Lancaster, PA: Lancaster Press.

Shewhart, W. (1980). *Economic control for quality of manufactured product.* Milwaukee: ASQC Press. (Original work published 1931)

Smith, A. (1997). *The wealth of nations: Books I – III.* New York: Penguin Books. (Original work published 1776)

Smith, H. (1984). *Beyond the post-modern mind.* New York: Quest Books.

Spedding, J., Ellis, R. L., & Heath, D. D. (Eds.). (1864). *The works of Francis Bacon* (Volume IV, W. Rawley, trans.). New York: Hurd & Houghton.

Stacy, R. D. (1996). *Complexity and creativity in organizations.* San Francisco: Berrett-Koehler.

Stern, R. N. (1996). Organizations and social systems. *Administrative Science Quarterly,41* (1), 146–162.

Taylor, F.W. (1967). *The principles of scientific management.* New York: W. W. Norton.

Van Buskirk, W., & McGrath, D. (1999). Organizational cultures as holding environments: A psychodynamic look at organizational symbolism. *Human Relations, 52* (6), 805–832.

Veblen, T. (1912). *Theory of the leisure class: An economic study of institutions.* New York: Macmillan.

von Mises, L. (1981). *Epistemological problem of economics.* (G. Reisman, trans.). New York: New York University Press.

Weick, K.E. (1979). *The social psychology of organizing.* Reading, MA: Addison-Wesley.

Weick, K.E. (1996). Drop your tools: An allegory for organizational studies. *Administrative Science Quarterly, 41* (2), 301–313.

Weisskopf, W. (1955). *The psychology of economics.* London: Routledge & Kegan Paul.

Weisskopf, W. (1971). *Alienation and economics.* New York: E. P. Dutton.

Werhane, P. H. (1991). *Adam Smith and his legacy for modern capitalism.* New York: Oxford University Press.

Whitehead, A. N. (1925). *Science and the modern world.* New York: Free Press.

Whitehead, A. N. (1966). *Modes of thought.* New York: Free Press

Whitehead, A. N. (1978). *Process and reality.* New York: Free Press.

Whyte, D. (1994). *The heart aroused.* New York: Currency Doubleday.

Wilber, K. (1985). *No boundary.* Boston: Shambhala.

Wilber, K. (Ed.). (1985). *The holographic paradigm and other paradoxes: Exploring the leading edge of science.* Boston: Shambala.

Wilber, K. (1995). *Sex, ecology, spirituality.* Boston: Shambhala

Wilber, K. (1996). *A brief history of everything.* Boston: Shambhala.

Wilber, K. (1998). *The marriage of sense and soul.* New York: Random House.

Wilber, K. (Ed.). (1985). *Quantum questions.* Boston: Shambhala

Wilber, K. (1997). *Eye of the spirit.* Boston: Shambhala.

Wiser, J. L. (1983). *Political philosophy: A history of the Search for order.* Englewood Cliffs, NJ: Prentice-Hall.

Wolf, F. A. (1984). *Star wave: Mind, consciousness, and quantum physics.* New York: Macmillan.

Wolf, F. A. (1996). *The spiritual universe.* New York: Simon & Schuster.

Wood, M. (1998). Agency and organization: Toward a cyborg- consciousness. *Human Relations, 51* (10), 1209–1226.

Zukov, G. (1989). *The seat of the soul.* New York: Simon & Schuster.

Index

www.ingramcontent.com/pod-product-compliance
Lightning Source LLC
Chambersburg PA
CBHW060635210326
41520CB00010B/1607